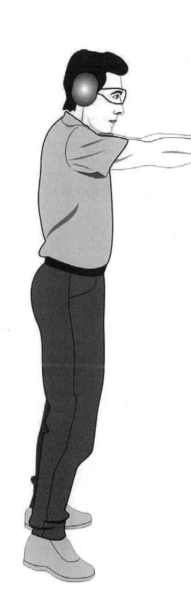

CANADIAN RESTRICTED FIREARMS SAFETY COURSE

Library and Archives Canada Cataloguing in Publication

Canadian Restricted Firearms Safety Course: student handbook - 4th edition

Also available in French under the title: Cours canadien de sécurité dans le maniement des armes à feu à autorisation restreinte, manuel de l'étudiant.

(*Également disponible en français sous le titre, Cours canadien de sécurité dans le maniement des armes à feu, manuel de l'étudiant.*)

ISBN 978-0-660-19824-8

Catalogue Number: PS99-2/1-2008E

1. Firearms--Canada--Safety measures.

2. Firearms ownership--Canada.

3. Firearms--Safety measures.

4. Gun control--Canada.

I. Royal Canadian Mounted Police (RCMP) / Canada Firearms Centre (CAFC)

TS532.2.C36 2008   363.330971   C2008-980104-0

This edition of the Canadian Restricted Firearms Safety Course is produced by:

Technical Documentation and Graphics Section
Information Management Branch/CIO Sector
RCMP Headquarters
Ottawa ON K1A 0R2 Canada
Fax: 613-825-9617

PREFACE

Acknowledgements

Many organizations with an ongoing interest in firearms safety volunteered their time to review and comment on this Handbook during its developmental stages. The efforts and assistance of the many people involved are acknowledged and appreciated. Without their help and that of the following organizations, this Handbook would not have been possible:

- Chief Firearms Officers and their Staff

- Central Forensic Laboratory – RCMP

- International Practical Shooting Confederation (Canadian Region)

- National Shooting Team (Olympic/Paralympic)

- Firearms Safety Education Service of Ontario (FSESO)

- Info-sécure Inc.

- Fédération québécoise de tir

- International Hunter Education Association (IHEA)

- Saskatchewan Association for Firearm Education (SAFE)

- Nova Scotia Hunter & Firearm Safety Education Instructors Association

- National Firearms Association (NFA)

- User Group on Firearms

- Coalition for Gun Control

Most importantly, the RCMP/CAFC wishes to acknowledge the talent and expertise of the certified Instructors of the Canadian Firearms Safety Course from across Canada, many of whom took the time and effort to provide written recommendations and suggestions in the development of this material.

Disclaimer

The improper use of firearms may result in serious injury. The material presented in this Handbook is intended to demonstrate the operation of firearms in accordance with safe handling techniques and an awareness of manufacturers' specifications and safety features.

The RCMP/CAFC makes no warranties whatsoever, either express or implied, oral or written, in fact or by operation of law or otherwise, regarding the safety of any firearm or the use of any safety mechanism shown in the Handbook.

Individuals should use their firearms in accordance with manufacturers' specifications and contact individual manufacturers as each model features different safety mechanisms and some of the techniques demonstrated might not be appropriate for certain firearms.

Ultimately, responsibility for firearm safety rests with the individual.

Table of Contents

List of Figures

List of Tables

	Name	Section
1.	The vital four ACTS of firearms safety	Introduction
2.	Evolution of firearms	1.1.10
3.	The vital four ACTS of firearms safety	2.1
4.	Types of black powder	3.3.1
5.	Ammunition safety points to remember	3.8
6.	The vital four ACTS of firearm safety	4.7.0
7.	Firearms hazards and precautions	7.6
8.	Social responsibilities of a firearm user (summary of)	7.7
9.	Some legal responsibilities of a firearm user	7.8
10.	Non-restricted firearms (classes of)	8.1.1
11.	Restricted firearms (classes of)	8.1.2
12.	Prohibited firearms (classes of)	8.1.3
13.	Ammunition	8.2.0
14.	Prohibited ammunition	8.2.1
15.	Prohibited devices	8.2.2
16.	The vital four ACTS of firearm safety	8.7

List of Charts

	Name	Section
1.	Sizes and types of handgun ammunition	3.4.2
2.	Typical cartridge names and actual diameters	3.4.4
3.	Dangerous range of handgun ammunition	3.5

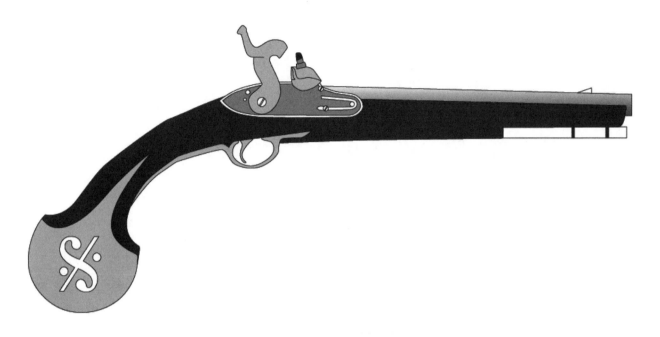

INTRODUCTION TO THE

CANADIAN RESTRICTED

FIREARMS SAFETY COURSE

INTRODUCTION

Introduction to the Course

The Canadian Restricted Firearms Safety Course (CRFSC) is designed to apply to novice restricted firearm users. Existing firearm safety courses across Canada have a proven track record in the reduction of firearm-related incidents. Most of these courses have been designed and delivered for firearms use in a specific activity. The CRFSC is an introductory firearm safety course intended for all new restricted firearms users and those individuals who wish to acquire restricted firearms.

Some information contained in this handbook is common to the Canadian Firearms Safety Course and other similar programs.

Individuals who wish to acquire non-restricted firearms must take the Canadian Firearms Safety Course and/or pass the tests. Individuals wishing to acquire restricted firearms must take both the Canadian Firearms Safety Course and the Canadian Restricted Firearms Safety Course and/or pass both tests.

The Canadian Firearms Program

The Canadian Firearms Program is administered by the RCMP/CAFC, which works with provincial Chief Firearms Officers and many community partners across the country in implementing the *Firearms Act* and its *Regulations,* and other related legislation regarding firearms.

The goal of the Canadian Firearms Program is the safe and responsible use of firearms, and it includes a range of activities directed toward achieving that goal:

- The **licensing** of all firearm owners and businesses

- The **registration** of all firearms

- The delivery of the **Canadian Firearms Safety Courses**

- **Public education** regarding safe storage, transport and use of firearms, and

- **Import and export controls.**

Licensing, registration and other Program information is recorded in the Canadian Firearms Information System, a national database that is managed by the RCMP/CAFC. Certain information is available to law enforcement agencies to help them prevent and investigate firearms incidents and crime, consistent with the public safety objectives of the *Firearms Act.*

Your personal information is carefully protected by the Canadian Firearms Program, consistent with the *Firearms Act* and its *Regulations,* federal and provincial privacy laws and other applicable statutes.

If you have any questions about the Canadian Firearms Program, please contact us:

RCMP/CAFC	
Telephone:	1-800-731-4000 (toll-free)
Fax:	613-825-0297
Email:	cfc-cafc@cfc-cafc.gc.ca
Address:	Royal Canadian Mounted Police / Canada Firearms Centre Ottawa ON K1A OR2

You can also consult the ***Firearms Act*** and its ***Regulations*** directly via the RCMP/CAFC website.

The RCMP/CAFC wishes you the best in following the Canadian Firearms Safety Course(s) for the class(es) of firearms you wish to acquire and/or possess. Please note that all Canadian Firearm Safety Course instructors and examiners must be certified by the Chief Firearms Officer for the province or territory in which you are taking the course.

Course Objectives

Firearm owners have social responsibilities. By completing this course, you will be instructed on what these responsibilities are. You will learn how to do the following:

- Handle firearms and ammunition safely.

- Use firearms and ammunition safely.

- Comply with firearms laws.

- Store restricted firearms and ammunition safely.

- Display restricted firearms safely.

- Transport restricted firearms safely.

The Canadian Restricted Firearms Safety Course consists of two parts. One is classroom instruction. The other is learning the material in this handbook. There will be both written and practical examinations. Passing them will demonstrate the knowledge and skills you have gained in the course. Live firing exercises, however, are not offered as part of this course.

During the course, some topics are discussed and explored several times. This will help you learn and retain the content. Leaving anything out of the course will reduce the amount you learn. This applies to all assignments, exercises or examinations given by your instructor.

The course emphasizes safe storage, display, transportation, handling, and use of restricted firearms. But safety depends on more than just safe physical actions.

Safe handling must include greater knowledge of the firearms themselves, ammunition, and the laws and regulations related to them.

Course Handbook

Safety also relies on your attitude about responsible handling and use of firearms. Pay close attention to the section on legal, ethical and social responsibilities. The safety of the people around you depends on it. Your own safety depends on it, also.

This book is an essential part of the course. The other parts are the classroom lessons and practical exercises given by the instructor. Together they will help you learn how to safely handle firearms.

This book contains the following elements:

- The **Vital Four ACTS** of firearm safety
- A brief history of firearms
- Information on firearms and ammunition and how they work
- Instructions on how to pick up, handle and carry restricted firearms safely
- Descriptions of how to unload, load and fire restricted firearms safely
- Descriptions of correct firing positions
- Instructions on range safety
- Instructions on the care and cleaning of restricted firearms
- Examples of factors leading to firearm accidents and the misuse of firearms
- A summary of ethics and laws affecting firearm owners and users
- Information on how to store, display, transport and handle restricted firearms safely
- A glossary of firearm terms
- Appendixes

This is an introductory course. More information and training is available on the various shooting sports from their own qualified instructors, associations and local clubs. We recommend you contact them directly for further details.

Also, do not hesitate to contact provincial/territorial or local authorities for more detailed information on firearm laws and regulations in your area.

Consult the **Firearms Act** and **Regulations,** or a firearms officer for information on controls affecting firearm and ammunition manufacturers, dealers and museum operators.

The Vital Four ACTS of Firearm Safety

Your instructor will refer to many different safety rules and guidelines. But time and again, the instructor will return to four basic rules. Any time you hear of an accident occurring, you can be sure at least one of these rules has been broken. These rules are known as the **Vital Four ACTS**.

The first letter of each rule becomes a letter in the acronym **ACTS**. You may want to think of these rules as acts you must carry out.

Table 1. The vital four ACTS of firearm safety

The Vital Four ACTS of Firearm Safety
Assume every firearm is loaded. • Regard any firearm as a potential danger.
Control the muzzle direction at all times. • Identify the safest available muzzle direction. • Keep the firearm pointed in the safest available direction. • The muzzle of a firearm should not be pointed towards yourself or any other person.
Trigger finger must be kept off the trigger and out of the trigger guard. • Resist the temptation to put your finger on the trigger or inside the trigger guard when you pick up a firearm. • Accidental discharge is far more likely to occur if your finger is on the trigger or inside the trigger guard.
See that the firearm is unloaded - PROVE it safe. • Do not handle the firearm unless you can **PROVE** it safely. • Check to see that both chamber and magazine are empty. Do this every time you handle a firearm, for any reason. • Pass or accept only open and unloaded firearms. This is an important habit to develop.

PROVE Safe

 **PROVE it Safe:**

Point the firearm in the safest available direction.

Remove all ammunition.

Observe the chamber.

Verify the feeding path.

Examine the bore for obstructions.

The firearm is now unloaded and safe until it leaves the direct control of the person who unloaded and PROVEd it safe.

Section 1

INTRODUCTION

TO

FIREARMS

1 - INTRODUCTION TO FIREARMS

1.1 Evolution of Firearms

1.1.0 Overview

a. It was probably the Chinese who invented the first explosive powder. They used it in fireworks and rockets. It was also invented at about the same time (the 13th century), by the English alchemist Roger Bacon.

b. People in the Middle Ages quickly learned to use explosive black powder to launch balls or projectiles. They did this by igniting the powder behind a ball or projectile in a cannon (see Figure 1).

c. A cannon is simply a metal tube sealed at one end. Burning powder in the tube produces an expansion of gases. The gas cannot expand against the sealed end. When it expands in the other direction, it pushes the ball ahead of it.

d. A charge of gunpowder was loaded into the bore of early cannons. This was followed by some wadding and a cannonball. Next, some priming powder, or a fuse, was placed in a very small hole or port drilled into the firing chamber.

Figure 1. Cannon

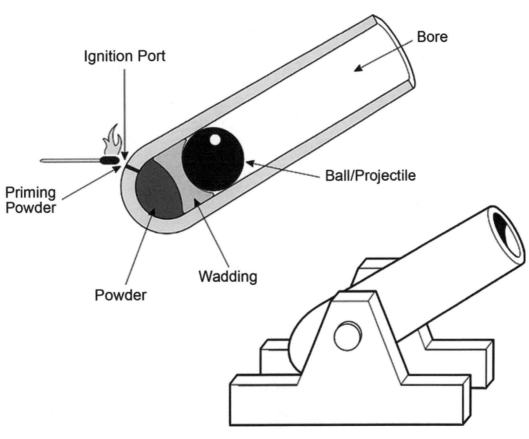

e. A burning wick, coal, or spark was touched to the priming powder. The flame travelled down through the port and fired the main powder charge inside the cannon. The explosion launched the cannonball.

f. The use of cannons changed how wars were fought. It also helped change the course of history. Stone castles no longer provided enough protection for the nobility and the villagers living within their walls.

g. During the following centuries, people developed firearms that could be carried and fired by one person. These early firearms had a smooth bore. They could shoot either single or multiple projectiles.

h. The development of these firearms brought about important historical changes. Their use on the battlefield marked the beginning of the end for armoured knights. Because these firearms could be carried, they were also practical for hunting.

1.1.1 Matchlocks

a. One of the earliest carried firearms was the matchlock. It was invented in the early 1400's. The matchlock (see Figure 2) made it possible for the user to aim and fire while holding the firearm with both hands.

b. A slow-burning match activated the matchlock. This match fired the firearm by igniting its priming powder. The match was held by a metal part, called the serpentine, which pivoted at one end.

c. Just below the lit end of the match was the pan. Its job was to hold the priming powder.

d. When the trigger was pulled, the serpentine moved slowly on its pivot. The end holding the burning match dipped it into the priming powder. The priming powder burning through the port fired the main charge of gunpowder in the barrel. The explosion of the main charge launched the projectile.

Figure 2. Matchlock

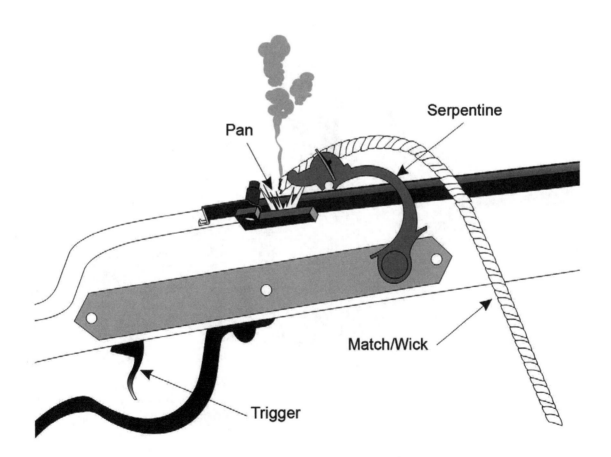

1.1.2 Wheel locks

a. The matchlock had many disadvantages. Rain or high wind could put out the match. Also, having lighted matches close to gunpowder led to many accidents. Two improved firing systems were developed in the 17th century. These were the wheel lock (see Figure 3) and the flintlock (see Figure 4 in Section 1.1.3).

b. The wheel lock firing mechanism worked much like a modern cigarette lighter. A strong spring turned a tooth-edged wheel against a piece of iron pyrite. This caused sparks. The sparks ignited the priming powder. The priming powder fired the main charge.

c. Between shots, the spring was wound up with a key, like a clock. This made the wheel lock ready for instant use, unlike the matchlock. The wheel lock was also safer.

d. However, the mechanism was complex and expensive to make. Also, winding was slow and springs often failed.

Figure 3. Wheel lock

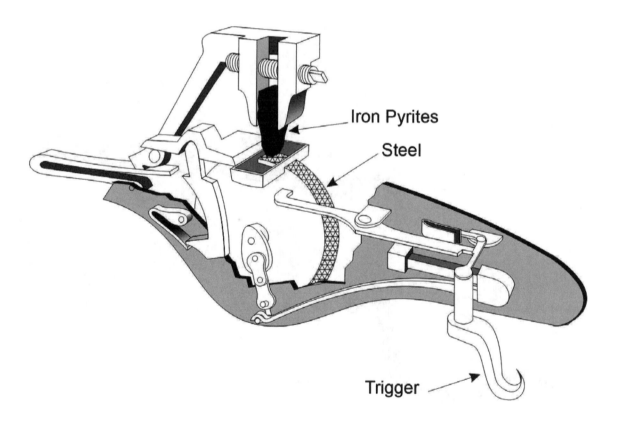

1.1.3 Flintlocks

a. The flintlock has an ignition mechanism similar to the wheel lock. It produced its spark by striking a flint against steel. Since it weighed less and was simpler and cheaper to make, it soon became more popular (see Figure 4).

b. It had a hammer-like part called a cock. Clamped to this cock was the flint. Opposite the flint was the frizzen or steel. When the trigger was pulled, the cock was released. A spring pushed it down to strike the steel with the flint. This produced sparks which fell into the priming powder in the flash pan. These sparks fired the main charge.

Figure 4. Flintlocks

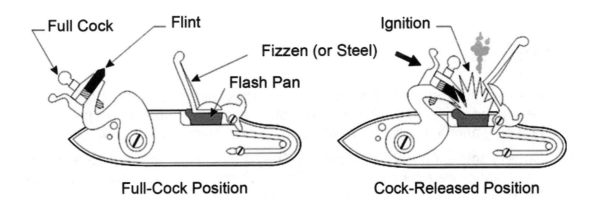

c. For centuries, flintlocks were the standard firearm (see Figure 5). During this time, many improvements were introduced. One such improvement of the flintlock over the matchlock and wheel lock was the development of a more reliable ignition system.

d. Other improvements included having more than one barrel, trigger and lock. This enabled the firing of more than one shot before reloading.

Figure 5. Flintlock pistol

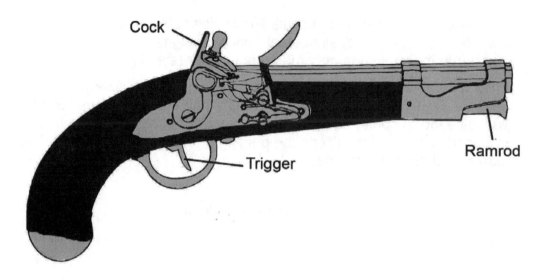

1.1.4 Pistols

a. Between the 15th and 17th centuries, firearms with much shorter barrels were developed. These could be fired with one hand. They were called pistols, probably after the Italian town of Pistoia where many were made.

b. Cavalry soldiers mainly used pistols. They did not need long-range accuracy. Also, pistols were far easier to handle than long guns on the back of a horse. Several could be carried, allowing multiple shots.

c. As new firing mechanisms were developed for long guns, pistols also began using them. Pistols eventually evolved into the various types of modern handguns.

1.1.5 Muskets

a. Muskets were longer-barrelled firearms. They were more accurate at longer ranges than pistols.

b. Muskets usually had smooth bores and could fire either single bullets or a charge of pellets. These pellets were called shot, similar to the projectiles fired by modern shotguns.

1.1.6 Rifles

a. Later, firearms with internally grooved barrels were produced. These were the first rifles.

b. The spiralled-barrel grooving, called rifling, caused the projectile to spin. This improved its stability and accuracy in flight.

c. Rifling was also used in some of the later muzzleloading pistols.

1.1.7 Percussion Caps

a. The percussion cap was developed in the early 1800s (see Figure 6). It was a small metal case (cap) containing material that would explode when struck.

b. When loading the firearm, a percussion cap was placed on a nipple located over the priming port. When struck by the hammer, the cap exploded, igniting the main powder charge through a hole in the nipple.

c. Percussion caps were far more dependable than flintlocks, particularly during stormy weather. They also permitted the development of the first repeating firearms by allowing one trigger and one hammer to discharge multiple barrels.

Figure 6. Percussion cap on a lock

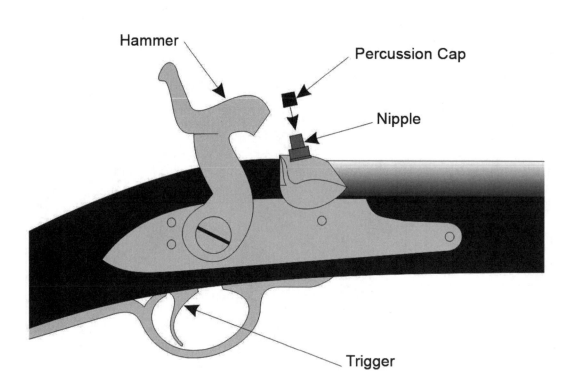

1.1.8 Cartridges

a. All early firearms were muzzleloaders. They loaded through the muzzle. But muzzleloaders were slow to reload. They were also restricted to one shot per barrel.

b. Attempts were made to develop firearms that loaded from the back. They were called breechloaders. However, these early attempts failed because the expanding gases from the burning powder charge leaked back through the breech parts.

c. In the mid 1800s, various cartridge types were developed that made breechloading practical. Eventually, metal cased cartridges similar to modern ones were created (see Figure 7).

Figure 7. Examples of modern cartridges

d. These cartridges contained the bullet or shot, the main powder charge, and the primer in one package. Pulling the firearm trigger caused the firing pin to strike the primer. The flash from the primer ignited the powder charge. The burning charge caused the cartridge casing to expand. This sealed the breech to prevent gas leakage. The expanding gas launched the projectile down the barrel.

e. Cartridges had at least four advantages:

   1. They were easily loaded into the breech.

   2. The expanding case prevented gas leakage.

   3. They were largely weatherproof.

   4. They were more reliable.

f. Cartridges called shells were developed for use in shotguns. These too contain one or more projectiles, powder and primer in one container. In addition, a wad separates the powder from the projectiles. The cartridge casing may be made from metals or other materials such as paper or plastic.

g. Metallic cartridges and shotgun shells were easy to manufacture. Loading firearms also became simpler. This made repeating firearms practical.

1.1.9 Repeating Firearms

a. Some types of repeating firearms are listed below:

   • Revolvers

   • Manually operated rifles and shotguns with magazines containing extra cartridges

   • Semi-automatic firearms (the power generated by the cartridge chambers another cartridge after each trigger pull)

   • Full-automatic firearms, such as machine guns (firearms which fire continuously as long as the trigger remains pulled and the firearm has a source of ammunition)

See Table 2, which summarizes the main points.

1.1.10 Table 2 - Evolution of Firearms

Table 2. Evolution of firearms

Evolution	Main Features	Limitations
Matchlock (15th Century)	• Used lighted match/wick to fire priming powder • Muzzleloaded	• Match/Wick easily extinguished by rain • Match/Wick burns out • Dangerous around gunpowder • Clumsy • Slow reload • Match/Wick adjustment
Wheel lock (17th Century)	• Spring-driven wheel rubbed against iron pyrites to produce sparks • Muzzleloaded • Musket, pistol types and rifles	• Spring required hand winding • Iron pyrites wear out • Mechanism breaks • Heavy, slow reload
Flintlock (17th Century)	• Flint snapped against a steel surface to produce spark • Muzzleloaded • Rifling introduced • Paper cartridge introduced	• Flints wear out or break • Springs can fail • Slow reload • Number of shots limited by number of barrels
Percussion cap (19th Century)	• Small explosive metal cap replaced flint • More certain of firing • First repeating firearms	• Slow reload • Cap separate from powder and bullet
Metal cartridge (19th Century)	• Bullet, powder and primer all in one safe container • Simple, reliable, safe • Breechloading became easy • Smokeless powder introduced	• Requires special equipment to reload cartridge • Easy for unqualified persons to load into a firearm
Breechloading repeaters (19th Century)	• Holds and can fire multiple cartridges • Semi-automatics and full automatics introduced	• More danger of an unused cartridge remaining in firearm • More complex mechanisms

1.1.11 Firearms in Canada

a. Since the 16th century, firearms have played a role in the history and development of Canada. They greatly expanded the range and killing power for hunting. People were willing to trade large quantities of furs for firearms and ammunition. "Trade guns" thus became an important factor in the early fur trade. This, in turn, helped open Canada up to the world.

b. Hunting provided a major source of food. It was often critical for survival, especially in poor crop years.

c. Later, the need for hunting to provide food became less necessary for most people for survival. However, many people today still rely on hunting as an important part of their lives.

d. Many have also turned to target shooting. Today, numerous shooting clubs and associations exist. Their members shoot various types of shotguns, rifles or handguns. A wide range of targets from clay to paper also exists.

e. There are also many gun collectors.

1.2 Major Firearm Parts

1.2.0 Overview

a. To use a firearm safely, you must know its parts and understand how they work. The following is a brief introduction to the parts of a firearm. Their functions are explained in more detail in Section 4 - OPERATING HANDGUN ACTIONS.

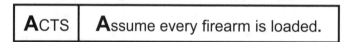

| **A**CTS | **A**ssume every firearm is loaded. |

b. Modern firearms consist of three major parts: the barrel, the action, and the stock/frame (see Figure 8).

Figure 8. Major firearm parts

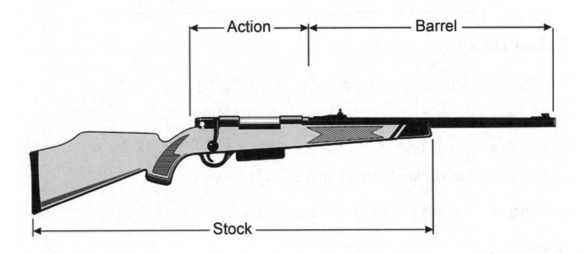

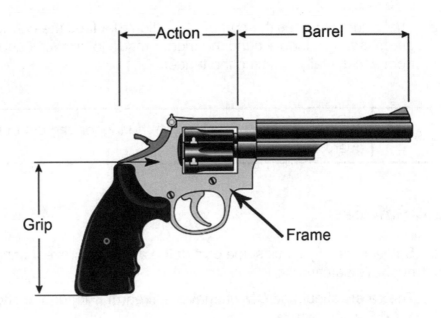

1.2.1 Barrel

a. The *barrel* is a tube, typically made of metal. The bullet or shot travels down this tube when the firearm is fired.

b. Often, manufacturers identify cartridge information required for that firearm on the barrel.

c. The opening at the end of the barrel from which the bullet or shot emerges is called the muzzle.

AC**T**S	**C**ontrol the muzzle direction at all times.

1.2.2 Action

a. The action contains the parts that do the following:

- Chamber the cartridge.

- Fire the ammunition.

- Extract the unfired cartridges and used casings.

b. *Triggers, safeties* and *magazines* are all parts of actions.

1.2.3 Trigger

a. The *trigger* releases the part of the action that fires the cartridge. The *trigger guard* is a rigid loop around the trigger made to protect it and prevent anything from accidentally touching the trigger.

AC**T**S	**T**rigger finger must be kept off the trigger and out of the trigger guard.

1.2.4 Safeties

a. Safeties usually block some part of the action to prevent firing. Some firearms do not have safeties.

b. The safety should be **ON** whenever a firearm is loaded. It should only be moved to **OFF** when required.

c. Some safeties may also act as decocking levers.

Never rely on the safety to prevent firing. A loaded firearm with the safety ON could still fire. All mechanical devices can fail; safeties can wear down and may not operate properly.

1.2.5 Magazine

a. The magazine is a device that holds cartridges in repeating firearms. The location of the magazine depends on the make and model of the firearm.

b. The magazine can be either fixed or removable.

1.2.6 Stock or Grip

a. The *stock* or *grip* is the handle of the firearm. Most are made of wood or a synthetic material.

b. Stocks and grips are designed to automatically align your finger with the trigger when you pick up the firearm. This is why it is so easy to accidentally put your finger into the trigger guard without thinking.

ACT**S**	**S**ee that the firearm is unloaded - PROVE it safe.

1.3 The Firing Sequence

a. Just about all modern firearms follow the same firing sequence (see Figure 9):

1. A squeeze on the trigger releases the firing mechanism. This results in the firing pin striking the primer of the cartridge.

2. When struck by the firing pin, the primer explodes. This projects a flame into the cartridge body.

3. The flame from the primer ignites the powder. The powder burns and produces rapidly expanding gases.

4. The high-pressure gas drives the bullet or shot forward down the barrel.

Figure 9. Firing sequence

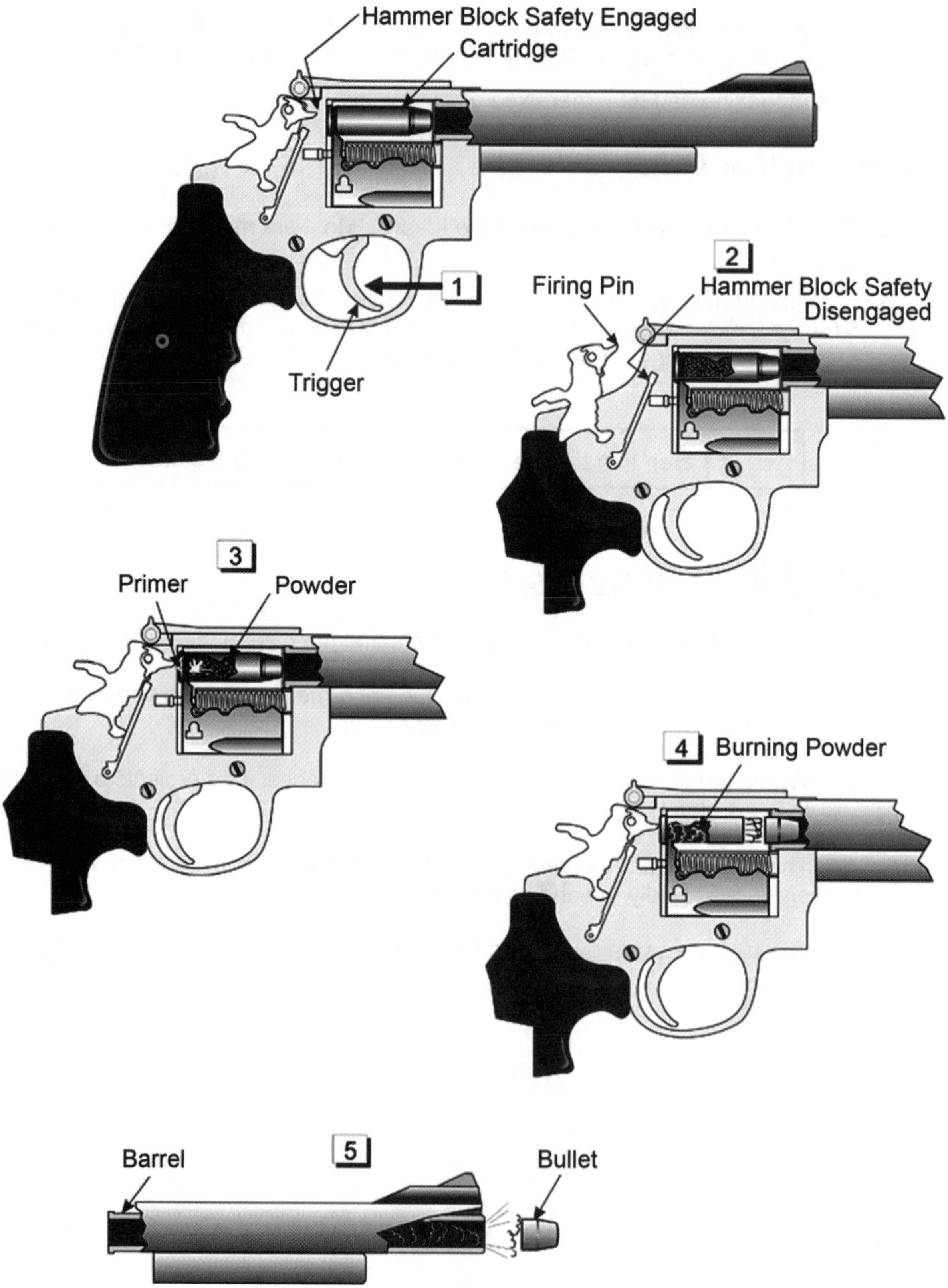

Hammer Block Safety Engaged
Cartridge
1
Trigger

2
Firing Pin
Hammer Block Safety Disengaged

3
Primer   Powder

4   Burning Powder

5
Barrel   Bullet

1.4 Types of Firearms

a. Firearms vary in design, depending on their purpose. One example is target shooting. The common types of firearms are as follows:

- Shotguns

- Rifles

- Handguns

b. The basic types of action (see Figure 10) used in these firearms are as follows:

- Revolving action

- Semi-automatic action

- Hinge (or break) action

- Bolt action

Figure 10. Common types of handgun actions

Single Action Revolver

Double Action Revolver

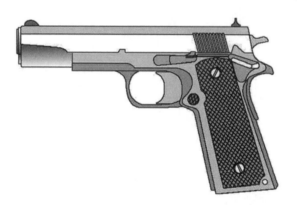

Single Action Semi-Automatic

Double Action Semi-Automatic

Figure 11. Other types of handgun actions

Break Action

Black Powder Revolver

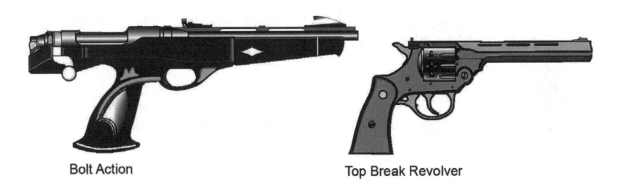

Bolt Action

Top Break Revolver

1.5 Legal Responsibilities

a. Various laws, regulations and restrictions govern your activities as an owner or user of a firearm. They set minimum standards of conduct, and you have a responsibility to know, understand and obey them.

1.6 Classes of Firearms

a. The classes of firearms are as follows:

- Non-restricted

- Restricted

- Prohibited

b. Legal requirements for a particular firearm depend on the class to which it belongs. Prohibited firearms are subject to the most stringent controls, restricted firearms are controlled to a lesser extent and non-restricted firearms are the least regulated of the three classes.

c. Although most airguns are not included in the provisions of the *Firearms Act*, they must be treated as firearms in respect of safe practices, such as the **Vital Four ACTS.**

 The Vital Four ACTS of firearm safety apply to all classes of firearms.

1.7 Review Questions

1. What are two differences between muzzleloaders and modern firearm designs?

2. List some advantages of modern cartridges.

3. What are the three major parts of a firearm?

4. What are the three classes of firearms?

NOTES:

Section 2

BASIC

FIREARM SAFETY

2 - BASIC FIREARM SAFETY

2.1 The Vital Four ACTS

a. Almost all firearm accidents can be prevented by following some basic safety rules.

b. The most important of these are the **Vital Four ACTS** (see Table 3). You may want to think of these rules as acts you must carry out.

Table 3. The vital four ACTS of firearm safety

	The Vital Four ACTS of Firearm Safety
☞	**A**ssume every firearm is loaded. • Regard any firearm as a potential danger.
☞	**C**ontrol the muzzle direction at all times. • Identify the safest available muzzle direction. • Keep the firearm pointed in the safest available direction. • The muzzle of a firearm should not be pointed towards yourself or any other person.
☞	**T**rigger finger must be kept off the trigger and out of the trigger guard. • Resist the temptation to put your finger on the trigger or inside the trigger guard when you pick up a firearm. • Accidental discharge is far more likely to occur if your finger is on the trigger or inside the trigger guard.
☞	**S**ee that the firearm is unloaded - PROVE it safe. • Do not handle the firearm unless you can **PROVE** it safely. • Check to see that both chamber and magazine are empty. Do this every time you handle a firearm, for any reason. • Pass or accept only open and unloaded firearms. This is an important habit to develop.

2.2 PROVE Safe

PROVE it safe:

- **P**oint the firearm in the safest available direction.

- **R**emove all ammunition.

- **O**bserve the chamber.

- **V**erify the feeding path.

- **E**xamine the bore for obstructions.

The firearm is now unloaded and safe until it leaves the direct control of the person who unloaded and PROVEd it safe.

2.3 Basic Firearm Safety Practices

2.3.0 Overview

a. While many safety practices have been incorporated into the *Firearms Act* and *Regulations*, experienced firearm users often exceed those requirements by following some or all of the recommended safety practices listed in the sections below. These safety practices are summarized in Table 7 – Firearms Hazards and Precautions, in Section 7.6 (For specific requirements on storage and transport, see Section 8 - SAFE STORAGE, DISPLAY, TRANSPORTATION AND HANDLING OF RESTRICTED FIREARMS).

2.3.1 Keep Firearms and Ammunition Separate and Secure When Not In Use

a. Some of the recommended safety practices are listed below:

- Firearms under your care and control are your responsibility 24 hours a day.

- Firearms are safer when stored and transported under lock and key. Examples include trigger or cable locks, and securely locked containers.

- In many cases, you are required by law to have your firearm unloaded and properly locked. Be aware of what the law says about which firearms need to be locked and when.

- Keep firearms and ammunition out of sight during transport and storage. This will reduce the chances of theft. It will also prevent unqualified or unauthorized persons from using them. Ammunition and firearms must be kept away from unsupervised children. Accidental misuse can cause a tragedy.

- Store firearms unloaded. Store ammunition separately. Lock the firearm and the ammunition separately when storing them.

2.3.2 Load a Firearm Only for Actual Use

a. Some of the recommended safety practices are listed below:

- A firearm should be loaded only when you intend to use it and where it can be safely and legally discharged. At all other times, it should be unloaded.

- Load a firearm only when you have reached the shooting area and you are ready to shoot. Completely unload the firearm before you leave the shooting area.

- Always make sure a firearm is unloaded before you pass it to anyone or any time it leaves your hands. Whenever possible, leave the action open.

- Never accept a loaded firearm from anyone.

- Always unload a firearm before transport or storage. This prevents accidental discharge if the firearm is bumped during transport. It also reduces the chances of unexpected firing by an unqualified user.

2.3.3 Be Sure Before You Shoot

a. Some of the recommended safety practices are listed below:

- Always use your firearm in the safest manner possible. Be sure of your target and beyond before you shoot.

- Always examine the bore for obstructions before loading.

- Always check that you are using the right ammunition. Use only the ammunition for which the firearm was designed. Carry only the type of ammunition you intend to shoot.

- Never rely on the firearm's safety. Safeties wear down and may not work properly. Also, a loaded firearm may fire even with the safety on. All mechanical devices can fail.

2.3.4 Be Sure of Your Target and Beyond

a. To be sure of your target and beyond, follow the recommendations below:

- Positively identify your target. Make sure it is exactly what you want to shoot.

- Do not shoot when in doubt.

- Check that the area behind your target is safe before shooting.

- Never use a scope as a substitute for binoculars to identify persons or objects.

b. Always be aware of where your bullet or shot may end up. This is your responsibility. A bullet or shot may ricochet. It may also travel far beyond the target. If unsure, never shoot if your bullet may hit a hard surface or water. Both can cause a bullet or fragments to ricochet in unsafe directions.

2.4 Secure Locking Devices

a. Secure locking devices prevent a firearm from being fired (see Figure 12). In some cases, they are required by law (see Section 8 - SAFE STORAGE, DISPLAY, TRANSPORTATION AND HANDLING OF RESTRICTED FIREARMS).

b. To work effectively, they must be installed properly. Please note that not all secure locking devices are compatible with each firearm. Several devices are available for this purpose. The most common are key and combination trigger locks, and chain or cable locks. All of these locks block operation. Check with a firearms dealer for a locking device best suited for your specific firearm.

Figure 12. Various firearm locking devices

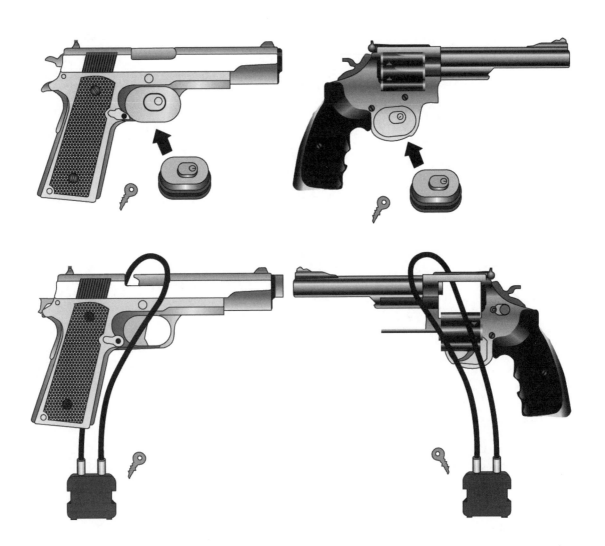

2.5 Review Questions

1. State the **Vital Four ACTS** of firearm safety in the correct order.

2. When you have ammunition in the home, how should it be stored?

3. Why is it necessary to store a firearm and its ammunition separately?

4. What are the minimum legal storage procedures for a restricted / prohibited firearm?

NOTES:

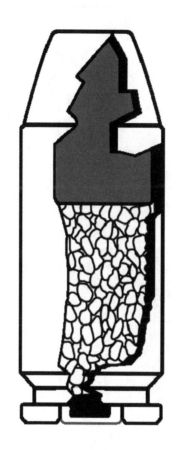

Section 3

AMMUNITION

3 - AMMUNITION

3.0 Overview

a. This section discusses black powder and handgun cartridges. This will help you choose the right ammunition. You should only carry ammunition that suits the firearm you are using and the target you intend to shoot.

For more detailed information, consult a firearms dealer or a gunsmith.

3.1 Rifling

a. Rifled barrels have a series of spiral grooves inside the barrel. The ridges of metal between the grooves are called lands. The lands and grooves together make up the rifling (see Figure 13).

b. Rifling makes the bullet spin as it leaves the barrel so it will be stable in flight.

3.2 Calibre

a. Rifled firearms are sized by calibre. Calibre is a measurement of bore diameter in either hundredths of an inch (Imperial) or millimetres (Metric). The distance could be measured either in inches or millimetres from land to land or from groove to groove, depending on the specific cartridge (see Figure 13).

Figure 13. Rifled versus smooth-bore barrels

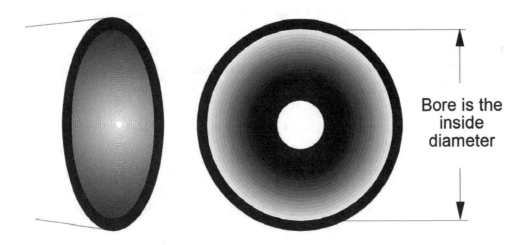

Rifled Barrel

Smooth-Bore Barrel

3.3 Black Powder and Projectiles

3.3.1 Black Powder

a. Muzzleloading firearms use black powder and lead balls as ammunition. There are also black powder substitutes.

b. Black powder is available in four different types (see Table 4).

Table 4. Types of black powder

Types of Black Powder	
Fg	Very coarse granules of powder. Used in larger-bore muskets.
FFg	Finer granules than the Fg. Used in muzzleloading shotguns, big-bore rifles and single-shot pistols of .45 calibre and up.
FFFg	Finer granules than the FFg and the most common type. Used in nearly all cap and ball revolvers.
FFFFg	The finest granules. Used only in the priming pans of flintlocks.

Never use FFFFg powder as anything other than a priming powder. Black powder ignites easily. Always handle with extreme care and wear eye protection. Never have a source of ignition around powder. Never smoke near black powder. Glowing embers may be present in the bore after firing a black powder firearm. An explosion hazard could be created if you proceed immediately to reload. Never interchange smokeless powder and black powder. Use them only in firearms intended for their use.

c. Remember, the finer the granules of powder, the more pressure it creates when fired.

d. Black powder ignites very easily. A glowing coal, a spark, even static electricity or a sharp blow may ignite it. Handle black powder with great care, especially when transporting it. Black powder should be stored in a secure, cool, dry place, and always in its original container.

e. As black powder ages, it becomes more unstable. When stored for long periods, the granules will begin to cake together and white crystals will form. When this happens, the black powder has become very unstable. It should be soaked immediately in water.

3.3.2 Black Powder Projectiles

a. Modern black powder or muzzleloading firearms shoot several different types (see Figure 14) of projectiles as follows:

- Spherical - a round ball, usually loaded along with a lubricated patch, which seals the barrel around the ball

- Conical - cylindrical-shaped projectiles known as Mini-balls, they have a hollow base that expands to seal the gases when the firearm fires

- Shot - pellets of assorted sizes and materials

- Sabot - plastic or synthetic carrier that encases a projectile.

Figure 14. Ammunition components for a muzzleloader

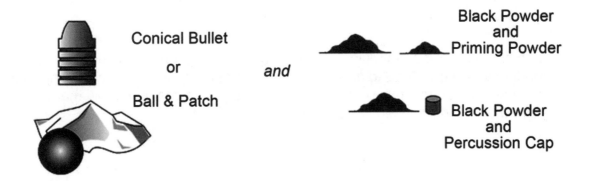

3.4 Cartridges

3.4.0 Overview

a. A cartridge is the ammunition used in a firearm. Two kinds of cartridges commonly available are: rim-fire and centre-fire. These terms describe where the primer is located at the base of the cartridge casing. They also describe where the firing pin strikes.

b. Manufacturers produce firearms of many calibres. Always make sure the cartridge name on the head stamp (see Figure 15) matches the information in the data stamp, on the barrel or slide of the firearm, if available (see Figure 16). This is the most important point to remember. Then choose the right type of ammunition for your firearm and target. The right shape or weight of the bullet is an example. If in doubt, consult a firearms or ammunition dealer.

c. If there is no data stamp, take the firearm to a qualified individual. They can measure the chamber and advise on proper ammunition. Additional information is available from manufacturers' catalogues and brochures.

d. Many firearm owners load their own centre-fire ammunition. This allows them to save money and create a high quality product made specifically for their firearm and shooting conditions.

e. Incorrectly loaded ammunition may cause the firearm to malfunction or jam. Malfunctions could lead to an accident. The firearm could blow up and injure the shooter. Do not accept or use reloaded cartridges unless you know that they were made and reloaded correctly.

Figure 15. Example of a rim-fire and centre-fire cartridge with head stamp

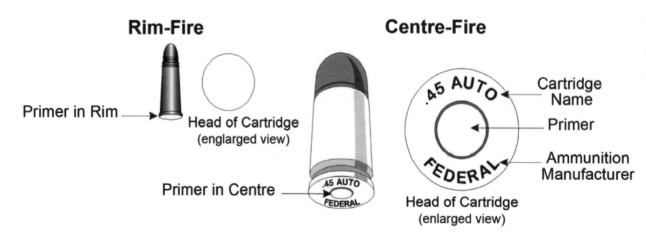

Figure 16. Example of a barrel data stamp

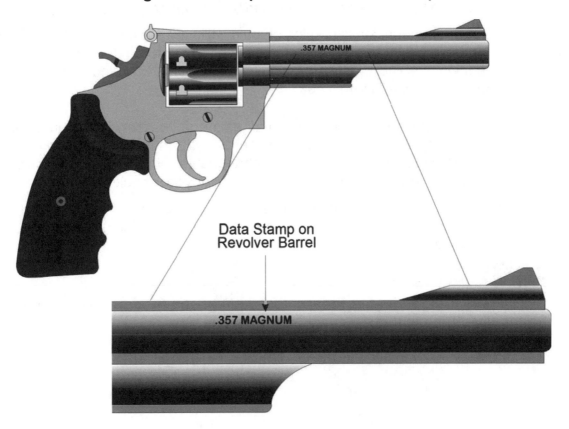

Data Stamp on
Revolver Barrel

.357 MAGNUM

Some firearms may not have a data stamp. Or they may have an incorrect stamp. Some firearms may have been altered and the existing data stamp may be incorrect. They should be checked by a qualified individual before use. If you are reloading your own ammunition, you must strictly follow the instructions and procedures outlined in the manuals provided for this process. Visually inspect all ammunition for defects before loading.

3.4.1 Types of Cartridges

a. There are two basic types of modern cartridges: rim-fire and centre-fire.

  1. **Rim-fire** ammunition 's priming chemical fills the space inside the bottom rim of a thin brass or copper cartridge casing. The soft rim dents when struck by the firing pin. This crushes the priming compound. It explodes, and ignites the powder (see Figure 17).

    • All popular modern rim-fire cartridges are .22 calibre. They commonly come in BB, short, long, and long rifle. A .22-magnum cartridge is also available, however, it is not interchangeable with the other .22 cartridges. Be sure to use the correct ammunition for your specific firearm.

    • Rim-fire cartridge bullets generally are made of lead. They are lubricated with grease or special waxes that reduce the build-up of lead in the handgun barrel.

Dry firing a rim-fire firearm can damage the firearm. Dry fire means to imitate live firing without a cartridge in the chamber.

Figure 17. Rim-fire cartridge

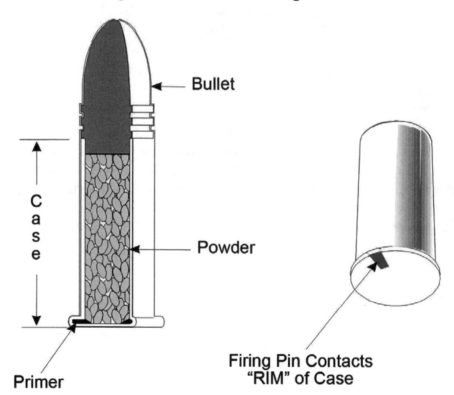

Bullet

Case

Powder

Primer

Firing Pin Contacts "RIM" of Case

2. **Centre-fire** ammunition (see Figure 18) is generally used for larger-calibre firearms. The primer is located in a separate cup at the base of the case. The firing pin strikes the primer. This explodes the priming compound. This in turn ignites the powder charge.

Figure 18. Centre-fire cartridge

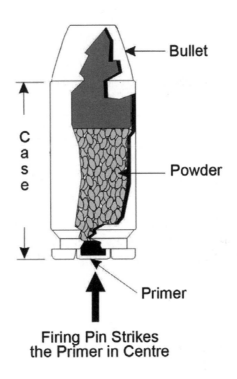

3.4.2 Chart 1 - Sizes and Types of Handgun Ammunition

Chart 1. Sizes and types of handgun ammunition

TYPE	COMPONENTS	PURPOSE	USES
Rim-Fire or Centre-Fire Sizes: Calibre e.g. - .22 or .45 or 9 mm	BULLET	Strikes target	Target Shooting
	POWDER	Burns and expands to propel bullet	Collecting Police
	CASE	Contains components	Lawful Profession
	PRIMER	Fires powder charge when struck by firing pin	Military

3.4.3 Cartridge Names

a. There are various ways of identifying or "naming" cartridges. Some cartridges have several names. The cartridge name, or an abbreviation of it, is stamped on the head of the case. It is also found printed on the ammunition manufacturer's box (see Figure 19).

⚠ Cartridges with different names are not interchangeable. (.38 S&W/.38 Special/.38 Super Auto)

b. Because a manufacturer may choose to make a firearm or ammunition in a cartridge originally made by another manufacturer, confusion can occur. For example, you can use a Smith & Wesson handgun to fire a .357 Remington Magnum cartridge made by the Federal Cartridge Company (see Figure 19).

c. The head stamp includes very valuable information, such as the cartridge name. It may also tell you the following:

   • The calibre

   • The manufacturer

   • Whether the ammunition is regular or magnum and any other relevant details

d. Always read the cartridge name. It is the only way to be sure that the cartridge matches the firearm. If in doubt, check with a gunsmith or gun shop.

e. The term magnum comes from the description of a large bottle of wine. It was first applied to large bottleneck cartridges that produced greater power than was the normal standard for that calibre. Today, it is more a marketing term than a technical term, but it is an important part of the name.

f. To choose the right ammunition for the type of target and firearm, follow the manufacturer's recommendations. For handgun ammunition, the manufacturer's recommendations are included in the catalogues distributed through sporting goods stores and gun shops.

Figure 19. Cartridge head stamp, data stamp and ammunition box label

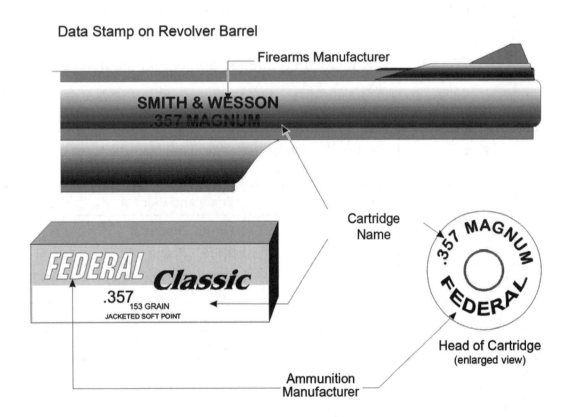

⚠ **Some ammunition may not have a cartridge name stamp such as rim-fire cartridges. Also, some privately reloaded ammunition may no longer match the original stamp. Whenever possible, refer to the information on the ammunition box. If in doubt, have any such ammunition checked by a qualified individual before you use it.**

3.4.4 Typical Cartridge Names and Actual Diameters

a. Chart 2 shows some examples of ammunition. As can be seen in the chart, cartridge names are often similar. Many different names may fit the same calibre. It is absolutely essential to read the whole name of the cartridge before you select it.

Chart 2. Typical cartridge names and actual diameters

Typical Cartridge Names and Actual Diameters			
Name	**Calibre**	**Bullet Diameter**	**Original Manufacturer or Major User**
.40 S & W	.40 cal.	.400"	Smith and Wesson
9-mm Luger (also known as 9-mm Parabellum, 9 mm x 19-mm NATO)	9 mm	.355"	Target Shooters Military/Police **Note:** 19 mm in the name indicates case length
.38 S & W	.38 cal.	.361"	Smith and Wesson
.38 Special	.38 cal.	.357"	Target/Police/Security
.38 Super	.38 cal.	.357"	Target
.357 Magnum	.357	.357"	Smith and Wesson
.44 Rem. Magnum	.44 cal.	.429"	Remington Arms Co.
.45 Auto or .45 ACP	.45 cal.	.452"	U.S. Government

⚠ **It is an offence under the *Criminal Code* for an individual to be in possession of prohibited ammunition. Never use incorrect ammunition in your firearm.**
- **Never use .38-S&W cartridges in firearms chambered for a .38 Special;**
- **Never use 9-mm Luger cartridges in a 9 mm x 21 mm.**

3.4.5 Cartridge Components and Materials

a. Ammunition varies in size, appearance and materials. Ammunition cartridges for handguns are made up of four basic components described below (see Figures 20 and 21).

1. The **bullet** is the projectile at the front end of the cartridge. It is propelled from the firearm by the expansion of gas from the burning powder. Usually, the bullet is made of lead or lead alloy. It may also be covered by a jacket of a harder metal. When the nose of the bullet is covered in this manner, it may be referred to as a full metal jacket, hard point or ball ammunition. If the lead is exposed at the front of the bullet, it is referred to as a jacketed soft point. Copper or gilding metal is commonly used as jacket materials.

    Bullets come in a variety of sizes, shapes and weights (see Figure 21). You must select the right combination for the target you plan to shoot.

    Target bullets are often made from lead alloy. Lead handgun target bullets are commonly of a design known as a wad cutter or semi-wad cutter. Their sharp edges produce precise holes in paper targets.

2. The **powder charge** is a chemical compound inside the case. It is ignited to propel the bullet through the barrel.

3. The **case** holds all the other ammunition parts. It is usually made of brass. It could also be made of steel, copper, or aluminum (see Figure 20).

4. The **primer** works in much the same way as a cap in a toy pistol. It contains a chemical mixture that explodes when the firing pin strikes it. This explosion ignites the powder charge.

Figure 20. Centre-fire bullet, powder charge, case, and primer

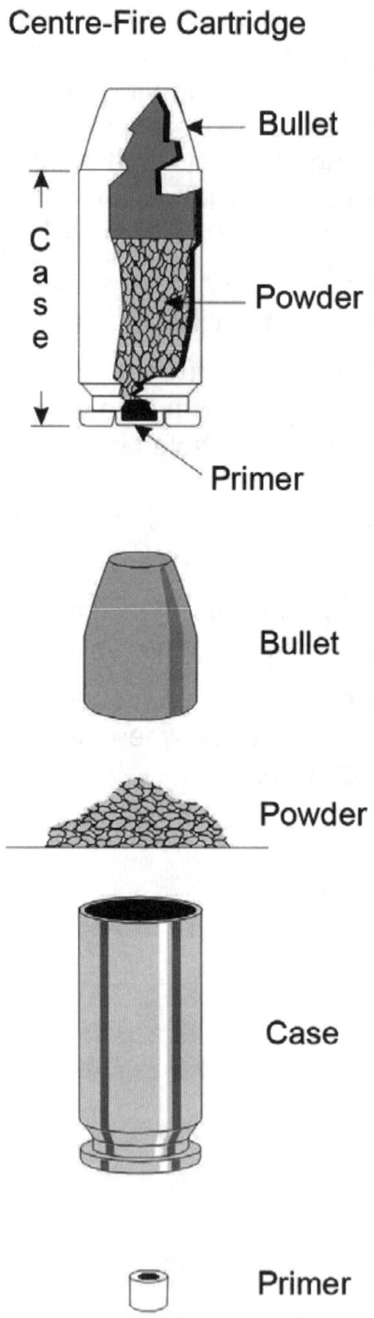

Centre-Fire Cartridge

Figure 21. Examples of handgun bullets

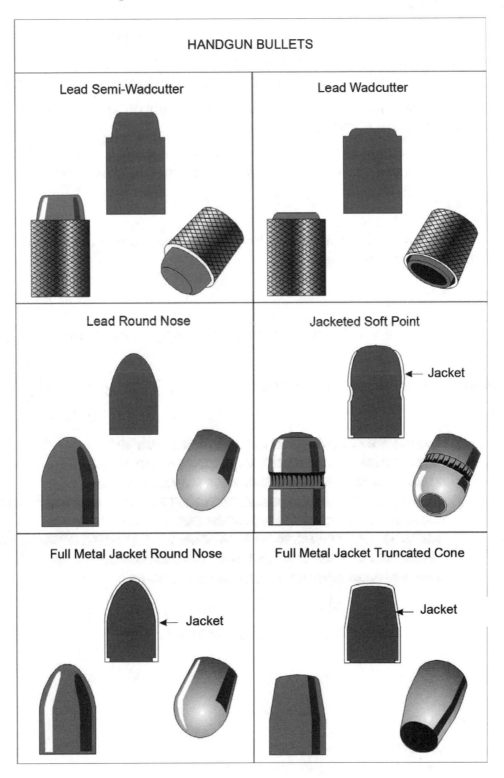

3.5 Ballistics

a. Ballistics is the study of projectiles in flight, and what affects them.

b. Modern firearms can shoot a long way. For this reason, every shooter should understand ballistics. Handguns can shoot a bullet more than two kilometres.

c. Ballistics tables for ammunition supply the information to calculate the flight path and performance of cartridges.

d. You want to shoot safely. Therefore, you need to know how far your projectile will travel. That means you need to know the **dangerous range** (see Chart 3).

Be sure of your target and beyond. If there is any reason your shot may be unsafe, do not fire.

Chart 3. Dangerous range of handgun ammunition

Dangerous Range of Handgun Ammunition	SOURCE: The Sporting Arms and Ammunition Manufacturers' Institute

Type	0 yd.	500 yd.	1000 yd.	1500 yd.	2000 yd.	2500 yd.
.22 Long Rifle (LR)						
9-mm Luger						
.38 Special						
.357 Magnum						
.38 Super						
.40 S&W						
.44 Rem.Magnum						
.45 ACP						
	500 m	1000 m	1500 m	2000 m		

Using Conventional Ammunition

3.6 Trajectory

a. Trajectory is the path a discharged shot or bullet takes during flight (see Figure 22). Several factors affect this path. These are gravity, air resistance, velocity, and mass.

   1. **Gravity** pulls the bullet down toward the ground as it is travelling forward. This results in a downward curved path.

   2. **Air resistance** slows down the flight of the bullet.

   3. **Velocity** is the speed at which a bullet travels.

   4. **Mass** is the weight of the bullet.

b. The firearm muzzle must be raised from the horizontal position to make up for gravity. The trajectory of a projectile is slightly curved. It often crosses the line of sight twice on the way to a target.

 Responsible shooters will follow the recommendations below:

- **Shoot only at targets within effective range.**
- **Consider how much farther the shot or bullet may travel beyond the target.**
- **Be prepared to be held responsible for where the bullet stops.**

Figure 22. Trajectory of a bullet

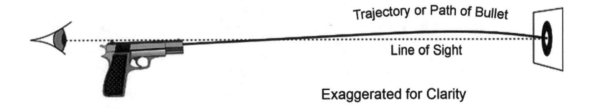

3.7 Hazards

a. The selection of the correct ammunition for the firearm is critical to safe operation but sometimes even the correct cartridge can fail to fire properly. Modern commercial ammunition is normally very reliable but there are several ways the cartridge may not fire.

- A **hangfire** is a delayed fire in which the firing pin strikes the primer but it does not create enough flame to ignite the powder instantly. If the muzzle is not pointed in a safe direction when the cartridge eventually fires, it may result in an injury. If the cartridge is removed from the chamber and then discharges, the explosive rupture of the case may also cause injury. Muzzleloading firearms may also have a hangfire.

- A **primer pop** (squib load) happens when the cartridge does not contain any gunpowder. The firearm will discharge the primer without the usual noise or recoil. This may have enough force to push the bullet out of the case, but the bullet may lodge in the barrel. If another bullet is fired, the barrel may rupture and cause possible injury.

- A **misfire** is a cartridge that does not fire. Misfired cartridges should not be reused in the firearm and must be disposed of properly. Muzzleloading firearms may also misfire.

If the trigger is pulled and there is no noticeable discharge, wait 60 seconds while pointing the muzzle in a safe direction. If there is no hangfire within 60 seconds, open the action and unload the firearm. PROVE the firearm safe to ensure there are no bullets lodged in the barrel.

3.8 Ammunition Precautions and Legislation

a. Explosives information is issued by Natural Resources Canada. It indicates that you may keep reasonable quantities of sporting ammunition on your property. "Reasonable" means quantities typically required for a rifle, handgun, or shotgun, or for part of a collection. This ammunition must be for your private use, not resale. Contact Natural Resources Canada for details.

b. You must take every necessary precaution against accidents by adhering to the instructions below:

- Ammunition must be stored out of children's reach. It must be kept away from flammables.

- Ammunition for a restricted firearm may only be stored in a place where it is not within easy access to the firearm, unless the ammunition is stored, together with or separately from the firearm in;

  - A securely locked container or receptacle that cannot be easily broken open or into; or

  - A securely locked vault, safe or room specifically built or adapted for the secure storage of restricted firearms.

- In a dwelling house, ammunition for a restricted firearm must not be displayed with the firearm and it cannot be within easy access to the firearm from which it can be discharged.

- In a place other than a dwelling house, ammunition for a restricted firearm must not be displayed with the firearm and it cannot be within easy access to the firearm from which it can be discharged, unless the ammunition is displayed in a securely locked container or receptacle that cannot be easily broken open or into.

- All ammunition should be stored in a cool, dry place. This will reduce the chance of corrosion or breakdown of ammunition components. These factors may cause the firearm to jam or misfire.

Keep in mind that storing ammunition in an unvented container may create an explosive hazard during a fire.

See Table 5 for a summary of ammunition safety points to remember.

Table 5. Ammunition safety points to remember

Ammunition Safety Points to Remember
• Carry ammunition only for the firearm you are using.
• Never experiment with unfamiliar ammunition.
• Using modern ammunition in old firearms may be hazardous.
• When a misfire occurs, slowly count to sixty while pointing the muzzle in a safe direction. Remove the cartridge following safe procedures. Then, carefully inspect the bore for obstructions.
• Never use old or corroded ammunition or reloading components.
• Never use military cartridges if you are not certain about their safe use.
• Never interchange smokeless powder and black powder. Use them only in firearms intended for their use.
• Store all ammunition so that unauthorized persons do not have access to it.
• Ammunition should never be displayed with a restricted firearm.
• Ammunition is most safely carried in its original container.
• When hand loading your own ammunition, be certain to strictly follow the procedures in the manuals about reloading ammunition. Treat primers with extra caution—they are explosive devices.

3.9 Review Questions

1. Is a 9-mm calibre smaller in diameter than a 10-mm calibre? Explain.

   no shit

2. What purpose is served by the grooves cut in the bore of a barrel?

   accuracy

3. What safety precaution should be taken for a firearm that does not have a data stamp?

   Bring to gunsmith

4. What is the maximum dangerous range of a modern handgun cartridge?

   2500 yds

5. Is it safe to use a .357 Magnum cartridge in a handgun chambered for a .38 Special?

   no.

6. Are very fine granules of black powder (FFFFg) used as the main charge in centre-fire handguns? Reason?

   no. Too fine

NOTES:

Section 4

OPERATING

HANDGUN ACTIONS

4 - OPERATING HANDGUN ACTIONS

4.0 Overview

a. To understand the safe use of firearms, you must become familiar with action types, how they work, and how to safely load and unload them.

b. This chapter first defines the different types of firearms, various safeties and action releases and shows how to do the following:

- Identify each type of action;

- Locate safeties (some actions will not open unless the safety is **OFF**);

- Open actions and unload – **PROVE it safe;**

- Safely load each type of action, with the safety **ON**, whenever possible.

Always wear safety glasses and ear protection when loading and discharging firearms.

4.1 Muzzleloading and Antique Firearms

4.1.0 Overview

a. Muzzleloading handguns are still in use today. However, most modern muzzleloaders are reproductions of older designs (see Figure 23).

b. This type of firearm is loaded through the muzzle. A measured amount of powder is poured through the muzzle into the barrel, followed by a patch, and finally a lead ball or shot. A hole located at the rear of the barrel just above the trigger allows a flash or spark to enter the barrel through the priming port and ignite the powder, firing the charge.

c. With flintlock muzzleloaders, the igniting spark is the result of the flint, held by the cock, hitting the frizzen. On percussion muzzleloaders, the flash is produced by the hammer striking a percussion cap.

d. Muzzleloading firearms use black powder or black powder substitutes. Black powder is classified as an explosive and is easily ignited by heat, friction, a hard blow, or even static electricity. It must be handled with **extreme care.** It is strongly recommended that individuals interested in muzzleloading seek additional training from qualified specialists in the field.

Older firearms should be inspected by a qualified gunsmith to be sure they can be fired safely.

Figure 23. Muzzleloader

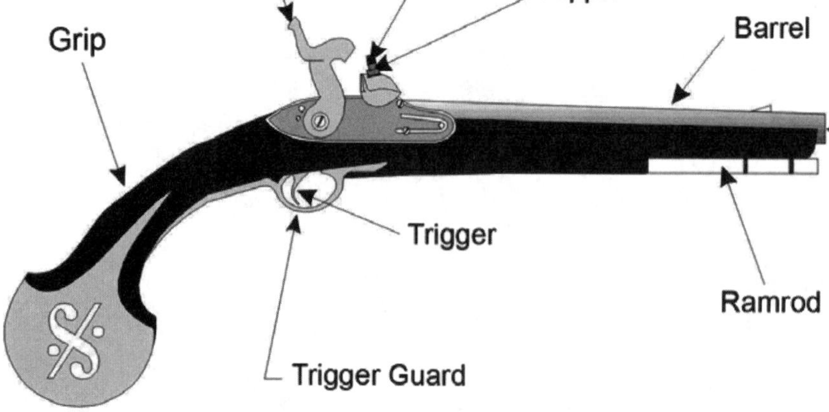

Percussion Pistol

4.1.1 Loading Muzzleloaders

a. Today, most firearms for black powder use are reproductions of muzzleloaders. Older firearms may not be safe to fire and should be checked by a gunsmith before use. If a muzzleloader is not primed to fire, it is safer to handle. To ensure that a muzzleloader is not primed to fire do the following:

- Point the muzzle in the safest available direction and keep your finger off the trigger and out of the trigger guard.

- Verify that the hammer is in the uncocked position.

- Check for the presence of priming powder in the percussion cap or in the priming pan.

- If the firearm is primed, remove the percussion cap or the priming powder.

b. In addition, it is difficult to tell if there is already a charge loaded into the barrel of a muzzleloader. Experienced shooters mark the firearm's ramrod at a level that shows the bore depth when the bore is empty (see Figure 24). When the marked ramrod is inserted in the barrel, it shows whether or not the firearm is loaded.

Figure 24. Correctly marked ramrod

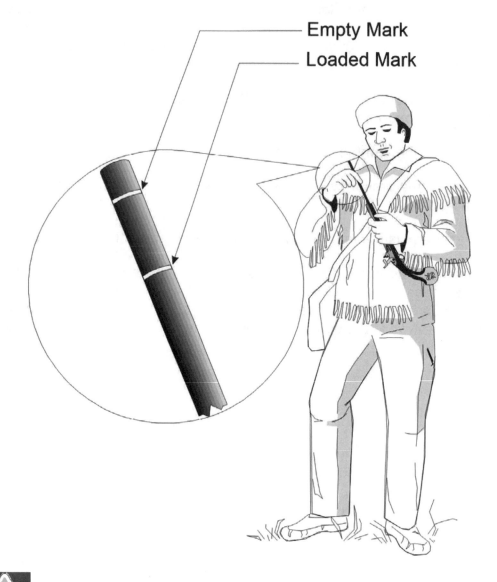

It is very important that exact loading and unloading procedures are followed when handling muzzleloaders (see Figure 25). Before attempting it, get the assistance of a qualified individual and carefully follow the instructions in your owner's guide. Ensure that the firing mechanism (lock) is rendered safe before proceeding to load the firearm. Before loading the firearm, use a rod with a tight fitting patch to check the bore, and fire a cap to remove oil from the bore and flash port.

c. In black powder revolvers, a measured amount of powder is poured into each chamber. A ball is firmly seated on each charge. Grease or lubricant is placed on top of each ball to lubricate its travel down the barrel and prevent "chain-firing" of all chambers. A percussion cap is put on the nipple of each chamber that produces the flash.

PROVE the firearm safe.

Figure 25. Loading a muzzleloader

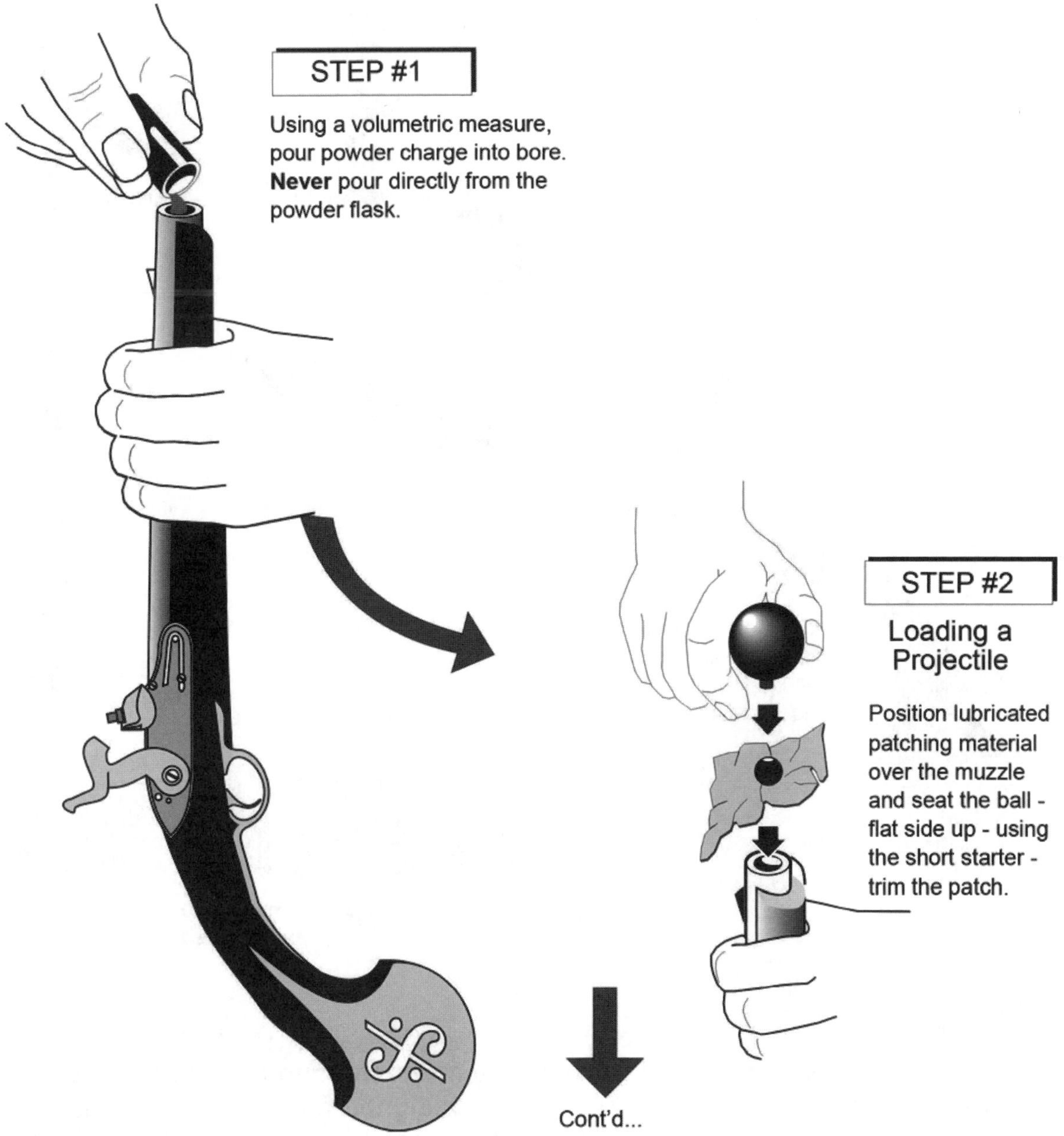

STEP #1

Using a volumetric measure, pour powder charge into bore. **Never** pour directly from the powder flask.

STEP #2

Loading a Projectile

Position lubricated patching material over the muzzle and seat the ball - flat side up - using the short starter - trim the patch.

Cont'd...

Figure 26. (Continued) loading a muzzleloader

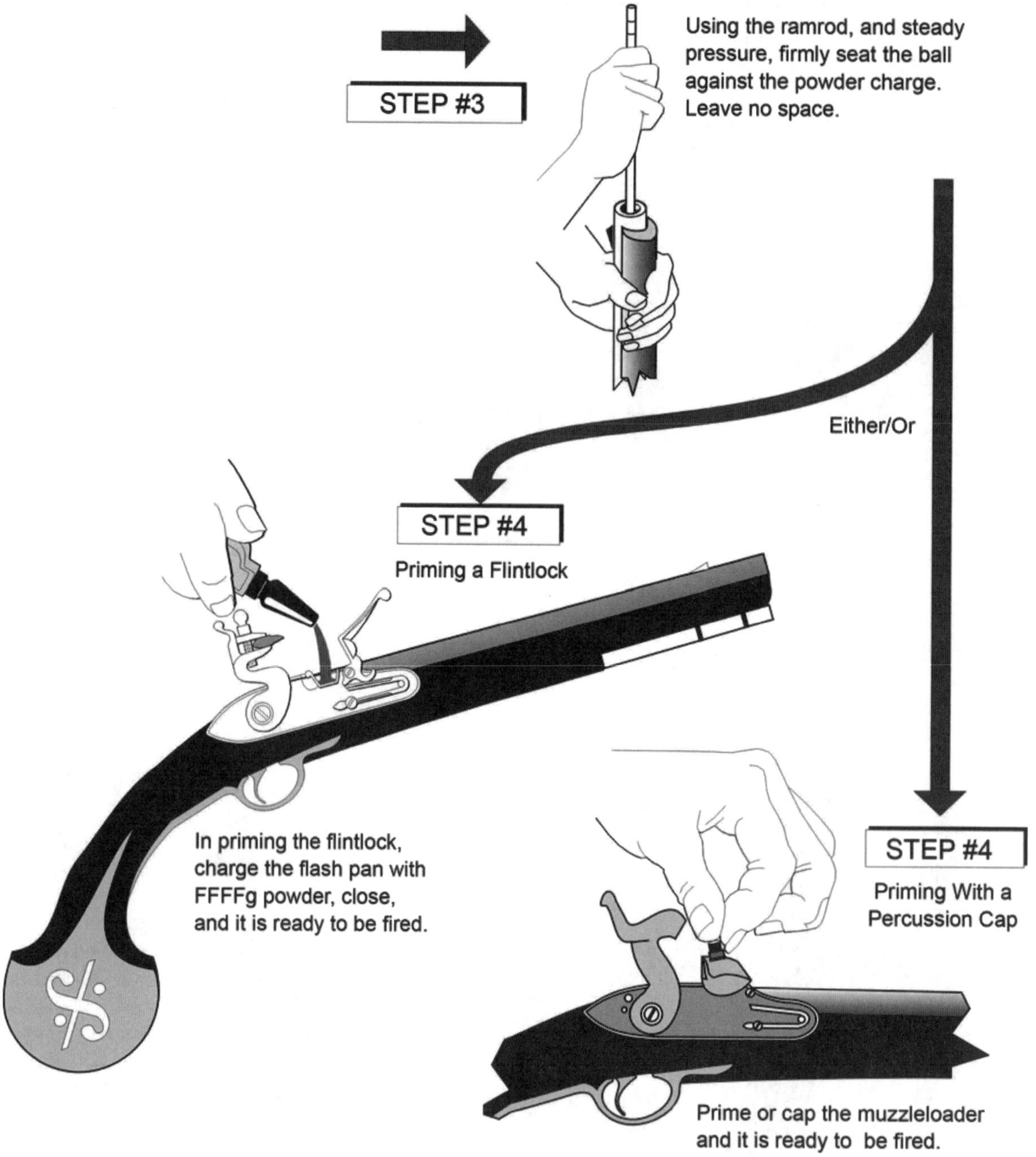

STEP #3

Using the ramrod, and steady pressure, firmly seat the ball against the powder charge. Leave no space.

Either/Or

STEP #4

Priming a Flintlock

In priming the flintlock, charge the flash pan with FFFFg powder, close, and it is ready to be fired.

STEP #4

Priming With a Percussion Cap

Prime or cap the muzzleloader and it is ready to be fired.

Never use smokeless powder in a muzzleloader. Never use black powder in a modern cartridge firearm not designed for it. Always use a volumetric measure to put powder into the muzzle; never pour directly from the main powder container. Under safe-storage regulations, black powder firearms are considered loaded when powder and/or ball are in the barrel.

4.1.2 Do's and Don'ts of Muzzleloading

- **Do** have old muzzleloading firearms dismantled, examined and declared safe by a qualified individual before using them.

- **Do** handle the muzzleloader with the same respect due all firearms.

- **Do** use ONLY black powder or black powder substitutes (i.e. Pyrodex) in your muzzleloader; never use smokeless powder.

- **Do** keep black powder far away from all cigarettes, matches or anything with an open flame, embers or anything that may cause sparks or heat.

- **Do** always use a powder measure to pour powder directly into the muzzle. Never use the powder horn or flask.

- **Do** carefully follow the manufacturer's recommendations for maximum powder charge.

- **Do** mark your ramrod to indicate when the barrel is empty and when it is loaded.

- **Do** wipe the bore clean of oil and excess grease before you load.

- **Do** make sure the ball or bullet is seated firmly on the powder charge.

- **Do** place grease in front of each projectile in a black powder revolver to prevent chain-firing.

- **Do** treat a misfire as a hangfire that could fire at any second. Wait at least 60 seconds with the firearm pointed in a safe direction.

- **Do** wear safety glasses and hearing protection.

- **Do** reseat your second charge after firing and reloading a single barrel on a multiple-barrel black powder firearm. Recoil can move the charge forward.

- **Don't** carry or handle a muzzleloading firearm with the hammer at full cock and primed unless you are ready to fire.

- **Don't** lean over or stand in front of the muzzle at any time.

- **Don't** load one chamber of a muzzleloading-multiple barrel or revolving handgun unless the percussion caps on the nipples of the other barrels or chambers have been removed.

- **Don't** store a muzzleloader with powder in it.

Black powder is also used in some metallic cartridges for firearms specifically designed for their use. Care should be taken. Although they have the same name as a modern smokeless cartridge, they may not be interchangeable. Never interchange smokeless powder and black powder. Use them only in firearms intended for their use.

4.2 Common Types of Handgun Actions

a. Handguns are generally classified by their type of action. There are two basic types as follows:

   1. A **revolving action** is used for some handguns (see Figure 27). It has several chambers in a rotating cylinder and can contain one cartridge in each chamber. Revolvers are manufactured as a non-swing-out cylinder, a swing-out cylinder or a top break.

   2. A **semi-automatic action** extracts and ejects empty casings and inserts another cartridge in the chamber automatically (see Figure 28).

Figure 27. Revolvers

Single Action
Revolver

Top Break
(Break Action Revolver)

Double Action
Revolver

Figure 28. Semi-automatic handguns

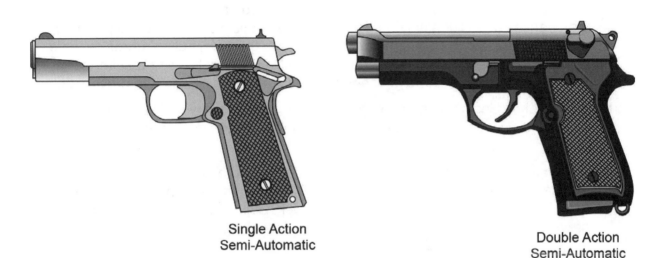

Single Action
Semi-Automatic

Double Action
Semi-Automatic

4.3 Other Types of Handgun Actions

a. A **hinge (or break) action** opens near the breech and is usually single or double barrelled.

b. A **bolt action** is similar to a door bolt and can be either single shot or multiple shot.

4.4 Trigger Functions

a. There are three primary trigger functions. They are single action, double action and double action only.

   1. A **single action** is an action that releases the hammer from a cocked position when the trigger is pulled.

   2. A **double action** is an action that cocks and fires with a complete pull of the trigger. Double actions may also fire as a single action.

   3. A **double action only** is an action that cannot fire in the single action mode.

4.5 Safeties

4.5.0 Overview

a. A mechanical device known as a safety is included on most firearms to reduce the chances of accidental firing. However, mechanical devices can fail. A hard blow may cause some firearms to fire even with the safety ON. Therefore, safe handling of a firearm by the person holding it will always be the most important firearm safety device. Always use the safety, but never rely on it to prevent firing.

b. The safety is designed to prevent the firearm from firing by interrupting the firing sequence. The safety blocks one or more of the trigger, sear, hammer or firing pin.

c. There are two types of safeties: manual safeties and built-in safety devices. Manual safeties can be placed on or off. They include slide safeties, like the lever safety, and frame safeties, like the safety lock. Built-in safety devices may prevent accidental discharge. They include decocking levers, trigger safeties, magazine disconnects and grip safeties.

Never rely on a safety to prevent accidental firing. A safety can fail. All safeties are slightly different. Check the owner's manual. Different manufacturers may use different terminology to describe their safeties.

4.5.1 Manual Safeties

a. The lever safety is found on either the right or left side of the receiver. It is operated by pushing forward and back to either the ON or OFF position.

b. The safety lock is normally operated by pushing it up into a notch on the slide. These safeties are commonly found on the left side of the receiver, near the hammer on single action semi-automatics.

c. With semi-automatic handguns, the hammer is automatically placed into the full-cock position each time the slide is pulled to the rear. In single and double action semi-automatic handguns, the hammer remains in this position. In double action only, the hammer returns forward to the rest position. In some models, it is not possible to have the safety on when pulling the slide back; on others it is. Whenever possible, when operating the action of any firearm, always have the safety on.

4.5.2 Built-In Safety Devices

a. With a double action semi-automatic handgun, there may be a **decocking device** or **decocking lever**. These are common on modern models. Instead of carefully manually decocking the hammer as you would with single action revolvers and semi-automatics, you need only depress the decocking lever. The decocking lever safely lowers the hammer. To accomplish this task, hold the firearm firmly in the strong hand and depress the decocking lever with the weak hand thumb. On some handguns, the decocking lever also engages the safety. Double action only handguns do not have a decocking lever.

b. The **trigger safety** is found on some models of handguns. This is a pivoting device found as a part of the trigger. As the trigger is pulled, the safety moves to the "OFF" position and the handgun can be fired.

c. Without a magazine in the handgun, the **magazine disconnect safety** prevents the firearm from being discharged.

d. The **grip safety** is usually found on semi-automatic handguns. It disengages when the firearm is held in the correct manner.

e. The **hammer block/transfer bar** will prevent the firing pin from touching the primer. On many older revolvers, the firing pin may rest on the primer of any cartridges directly below it when the hammer is in the forward position. If the hammer is struck, the cartridge will fire.

f. Most modern revolvers include a safety device to prevent this from happening. This is normally accomplished by preventing the firing pin from touching the primer unless the trigger is held all the way to the rear. The most common safety devices used to accomplish this are the **hammer block and transfer bar.** Check with your owner's manual or a gunsmith to find out if your revolver has one of these devices.

g. Safely **lowering the hammer from the full-cock position on a single action revolver** requires caution. The following method can be used when a cease fire is called and the hammer is at full cock:

    1. While maintaining a solid grip with the strong hand, place the weak-hand thumb fully on the hammer.

    2. Pull the trigger with the strong-hand trigger finger and begin to slowly lower the hammer fully forward.

h. There are some differences between various models of single action handguns. If possible with the model you are using, move the trigger finger off the trigger and out of the trigger guard immediately after the hammer begins to move forward. Slowly and carefully, lower the hammer. If there is no half-cock position, lower the hammer all the way forward and down.

Be very careful when moving the hammer. It could slip from beneath your weak hand thumb and fire the cartridge. Persons who are right handed would consider their left hand as their weak hand. The presence of a half cock on a firearm does not guarantee it is a safety. Some firearms do not use it as a safety. Check the owner's manual.

i.   Double action handguns also rely on a heavy double action trigger pull as a further safety barrier to accidental firing. Their trigger pull is approximately 6 kilograms or 13 lb. pressure, compared to a single action trigger pull of approximately 1.5 kilograms or 3 lb. Some specialized competitive firearms have much lighter trigger pulls, i.e. less than 0.5 kilograms or 1 lb.

Before loading any firearm, determine the ON position of the safety. Although all the illustrations of revolvers and pistols in this manual depict firearms with exposed hammers, many manufacturers produce them with internal hammers. Although some of these internal hammers function identically to the external hammers on comparable pistols, most function more like the mechanism on a bolt action. The hammer does not pivot on an axis; it moves back and forth in a straight line. It is called a striker. Some striker mechanisms use a built-in firing pin—others hit the firing pin and drive it forward. All the safety procedures for exposed hammers apply to internal hammers, but because the hammer is not visible, it is difficult to see if the hammer is cocked. Great care should be taken.

4.6 Action Releases

a.   Most handguns, other than semi-automatics, have some type of mechanism that must be moved to allow an action to be opened or closed. The location of the action release mechanism depends on the make and model of the firearm.

Do not touch any firearm unless you know how to handle it safely. If you do not know, get help from the owner's manual, or a person who knows that firearm well.

4.7 General Loading and Unloading Procedures

4.7.0 Overview

a. Before attempting to unload a firearm, first follow the **Vital Four ACTS.**

Table 6. The vital four ACTS of firearm Safety

The Vital Four ACTS of Firearm Safety	
☞	**A**ssume every firearm is loaded. • Regard any firearm as a potential danger.
☞	**C**ontrol the muzzle direction at all times. • Identify the safest available muzzle direction. • Keep the firearm pointed in the safest available direction. • The muzzle of a firearm should not be pointed towards yourself or any other person.
☞	**T**rigger finger must be kept off the trigger and out of the trigger guard. • Resist the temptation to put your finger on the trigger or inside the trigger guard when you pick up a firearm. • Accidental discharge is far more likely to occur if your finger is on the trigger or inside the trigger guard.
☞	**S**ee that the firearm is unloaded - PROVE it safe. • Do not handle the firearm unless you can **PROVE** it safely. • Check to see that both chamber and magazine are empty. Do this every time you handle a firearm, for any reason. • Pass or accept only open and unloaded firearms. This is an important habit to develop.

4.7.1 Unloading Procedure - PROVE it Safe

a. **PROVE** is an acronym, or memory aid, that stands for the five steps required to ensure a firearm unloaded and safe. The five steps are: Point, Remove, Observe, Verify and Examine. These procedures must be followed to safely unload any firearm.

   1. **P**oint the firearm in the safest available direction throughout the unloading procedure.

      • Make sure that nothing touches the trigger throughout this procedure.

      • Put the safety **ON**, if it can be left on during the unloading process.

   2. **R**emove all ammunition as follows:

      • If the firearm has a detachable magazine, remove the magazine from the firearm first. (This prevents a semi-automatic from chambering another cartridge if the action closes).

      • Open the action to remove any cartridges from the chamber(s).

      • Leave the action open.

   3. **O**bserve the chamber(s) to confirm that there is no cartridge(s) or empty casing(s).

   4. **V**erify that the feeding path is clear of ammunition, casings, or foreign objects.

   5. **E**xamine the bore for lubricant, rust, or other obstructions.

The firearm is now unloaded and safe until it leaves the direct control of the person who unloaded and PROVEd it safe.

4.7.2 Checking the Barrel for Obstructions

a. In all of the following loading procedures, **always check the barrel and chamber for obstructions before loading**. Whenever possible, this should be done by looking through the barrel from the **BACK** or breech end. If you cannot, be very certain the firearm is unloaded and the action is open and chamber empty **BEFORE** looking down the barrel from the muzzle end. Some shooters prefer to run a rod with a tight-fitting patch through the barrel before loading, rather than looking down the barrel. Use normal cleaning procedures to remove an obstruction, or take the firearm to an expert.

 Unless the patch fills the bore completely, obstructions may not be detected. Only load a firearm when you intend to use it, and only in an area where it can be safely and legally discharged.

4.7.3 Loading Procedure

1. Prepare the firearm for loading by going through the complete unloading procedure - PROVE it safe.

2. Clear any obstructions from the chamber(s) and bore(s). Clean if required.

3. Point the firearm in the safest available direction throughout the loading and chambering procedure.

4. Make sure that nothing touches the trigger throughout this process.

5. Put the safety ON, if it can be left on during the loading process.

6. Where possible, with the action open, select and load the correct ammunition by matching the data stamp on the firearm to the head stamp on the cartridge.

7. Point down range, extend arm, locking wrist and elbow, and close the action.

8. Leave any safety on (if applicable) until ready to fire.

The firearm is now loaded and read for use. It requires continuous care and attention until it is unloaded.

 Always be sure of your target and beyond.

4.8 Loading and Unloading the Most Common Action Types

⚠ All firearms may not be able to be handled safely by all persons, i.e. grip is too large, the slide lock is out of reach, etc. Do not attempt to handle any firearm that you are uncomfortable handling. To ensure proper fit of any firearm, seek the assistance of a qualified individual.

4.9 Operating Repeating Firearms: Revolver Actions

4.9.0 Overview

a. All firearms have their own unique aspects. One of the best ways to discover the specific methods for unloading and loading your particular firearm is to study the owner's manual. The steps outlined in this section are not meant to replace a full understanding of a given firearm owner's manual. The following information is an introduction to the most common actions. The general procedure does not change, but the details can vary significantly.

b. Many firearms are repeaters. Revolvers, for example, are repeaters because they hold more than one cartridge and can be fired several times in a row. The shooter must manually place another cartridge into the firing position. The most common manually repeating handguns are the revolvers described in this section.

c. The extra cartridges in a manually repeating revolver are contained in the cylinder (see Figure 29).

d. The revolving action takes its name from a revolving cylinder containing a number of cartridge chambers. One chamber at a time lines up with the barrel and hammer. Revolver cylinders may rotate either clockwise or counter-clockwise, depending on the manufacturer.

e. Most single action revolvers have cylinders that are incapable of swinging out. Cartridges are inserted and removed one at a time through a loading port, usually located on the right side. When firing the single action revolver, the hammer must be manually placed in the full-cock position for each shot. Pulling the trigger completes one function. It releases the hammer.

Figure 29. Single action revolver

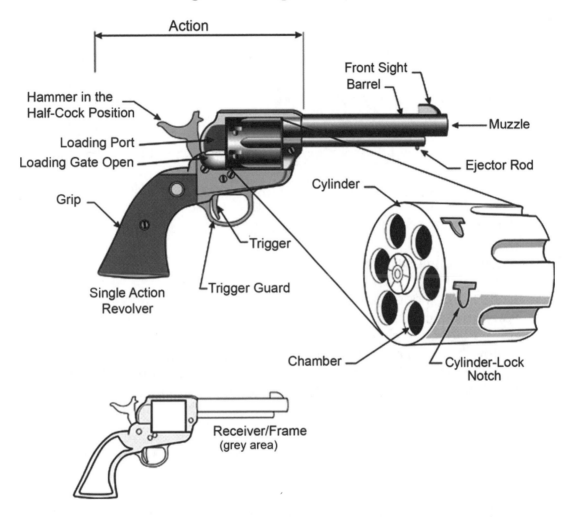

f. In a double action revolver, pulling the trigger all the way to the rear completes two functions:

1. Turns the cylinder so a cartridge lines up with the barrel under the hammer; and
2. Cocks and releases the hammer.

g. The cylinder normally has a release that enables it to swing out. This allows more than one cartridge at a time to be inserted, or ejected from, the cylinder.

h. Break open revolvers operate in a similar manner to other double action revolvers. Instead of the cylinder swinging out, however, the action hinges open, normally to the top or bottom.

4.9.1 Revolver: Single Action Non-Swing-Out Cylinder (Loading Gate) / Unloading Procedure - PROVE it Safe

 Before attempting to unload a firearm, follow the Vital Four ACTS.

1. **P**oint the firearm in the safest available direction throughout the unloading procedure:

   - Make sure that nothing touches the trigger throughout this procedure.

   - Open the loading gate and check if the cylinder will rotate. If the cylinder does NOT rotate, put the safety **ON,** hammer in half-cock / loading notch during the unloading procedure.

2. **R**emove all ammunition as follows:

   - Once the cylinder rotates, observe each chamber through the loading port, as you turn the cylinder, to ensure that there are no cartridges in the cylinder. If any cartridges or casings are present, use the ejector rod under the barrel to remove them. The chamber must be aligned with the loading port. Push the ejector rod from the muzzle to the breech. Let any cartridge or casing fall on the shooting bench or range floor and leave it there until you have completed all steps.

3. **O**bserve every chamber to confirm that there is no cartridge(s) or empty casing(s).

4. **V**erify by inspecting to ensure that the feeding path is clear or ammunition, casings or foreign objects.

5. **E**xamine the bore for lubricant, rust, or other obstructions.

The firearm is now unloaded and safe until it leaves the direct control of the person who unloaded and PROVEd it safe.

Figure 30. Removing a cartridge from a single action revolver

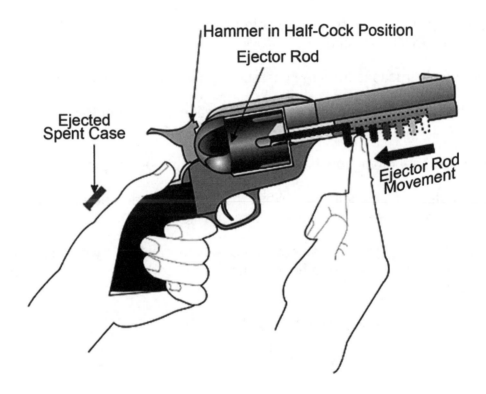

4.9.2 Revolver: Single Action Non-Swing-Out Cylinder (Loading Gate) / Loading Procedure

 **Only load a firearm when you intend to use it, and only in an area where it can be safely and legally discharged.**

1. Prepare the firearm for loading by going through the complete unloading procedure - **PROVE** it safe.

2. Clear any obstructions from the chamber(s) and barrel. Clean if required.

3. Point the firearm in the safest available direction throughout the loading procedure.

4. Make sure that nothing touches the trigger throughout this process.

5. Put the safety **ON,** if applicable. While most revolvers do not have safeties, some do. Check your owner's manual or ask a qualified gunsmith.

6. With the loading gate open, select the correct ammunition by matching the data stamp on the firearm with the head stamp on the cartridge. Insert the cartridge(s) into the chamber(s).

7. Close the loading gate covering the port.

8. Leave any safety on (if applicable) until ready to fire.

Always be sure of your target and beyond.

The firearm is now loaded and ready for use. It requires continuous care and attention until it is unloaded.

Figure 31. Loading a single action non-swing-out cylinder (loading gate revolver)

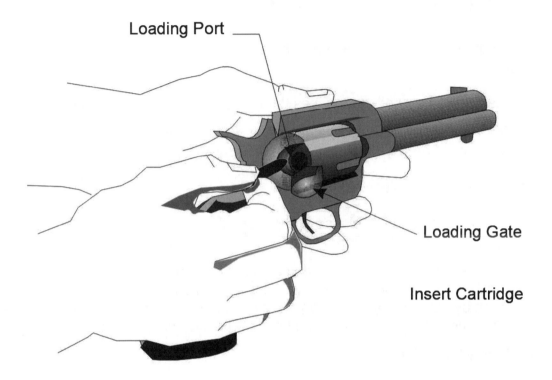

Loading Port

Loading Gate

Insert Cartridge

4.9.3 Revolver: Double Action Swing-Out Cylinder and Break Open / Unloading Procedure PROVE it Safe

 Before attempting to unload a firearm, follow the Vital Four ACTS.

1. **P**oint the firearm in the safest available direction throughout the unloading procedure:

   - Make sure that nothing touches the trigger throughout this procedure.

   - Put the safety **ON**, if applicable. While most revolvers do not have safeties, some do. Check your owner's manual or ask a qualified gunsmith.

2. **R**emove all ammunition as follows:

   - Operate the cylinder release and expose the chambers by swinging the cylinder to the side or top.

   - Tip the muzzle slightly upward in a safe direction and operate the ejector rod to allow the cartridges or empty casings to fall out. If not ejected, remove them by hand. Let any cartridge or casing fall on the shooting bench or range floor and leave it there until you have completed all the steps.

   - Leave the action open.

3. **O**bserve the chambers to confirm that there are no cartridges or empty casings.

4. **V**erify that the feeding path to make sure it is clear of ammunition, casings, or foreign objects.

5. **E**xamine the bore for lubricant, rust, or other obstructions.

The firearm is now unloaded and safe until it leaves the direct control of the person who unloaded and PROVEd it safe.

Figure 32. Double action revolver swing-out cylinder

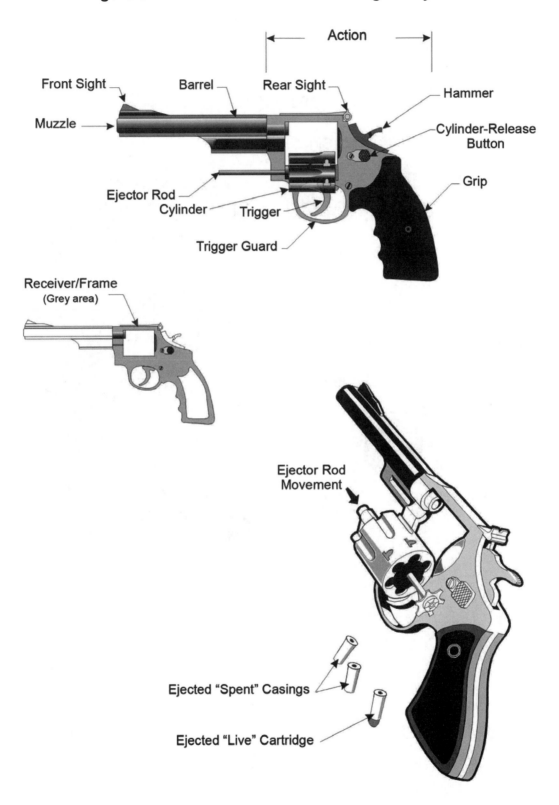

Figure 33. Top break revolver

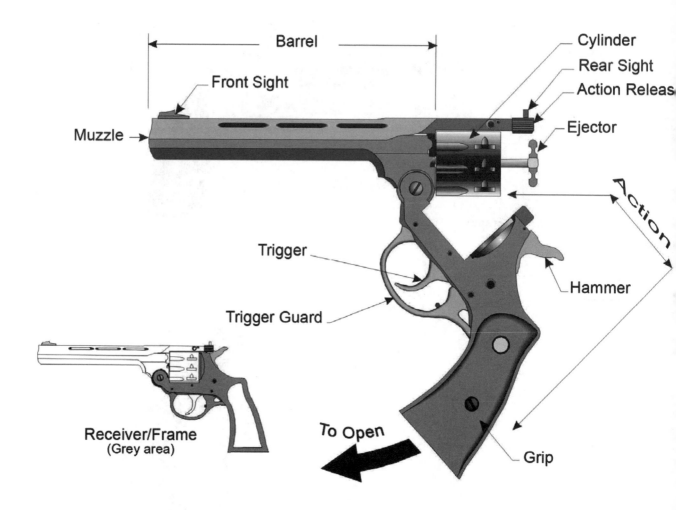

4.9.4 Revolver: Double Action Swing-Out Cylinder and Break Open / Loading Procedure - PROVE it Safe

 Only load a firearms when you intend to use it, and only in an area where it can be safely and legally discharged.

1. Prepare the firearm for loading by going through the complete unloading procedure - **PROVE** it safe.

2. Clear any obstructions from the chamber(s) and bore. Clean if required.

3. Point the firearm in the safest available direction throughout the loading procedure.

4. Make sure that nothing touches the trigger throughout this process.

5. Leave the hammer fully down during the loading process.

6. With the action open, select the correct ammunition by verifying that the data stamp on the firearm matches the head stamp on the cartridge.

7. Place the cartridge(s) into the chamber(s).

8. Close the cylinder firmly, locking the action closed.

9. Leave the hammer fully forward. Leave any safety on, if applicable, until ready to fire.

The firearm is now loaded and ready for use. It requires continuous care and attention until it is unloaded.

 Always be sure of your target and beyond.

4.10 Semi-Automatic Actions: Handguns

4.10.0 Overview

a. With each pull of the trigger, the semi-automatic action uses part of the energy of the expanding gas from the burning powder to extract the empty cartridge case and to chamber the next cartridge. No hand movement is needed to load another cartridge into the firing position. Each time a cartridge is fired, another cartridge is placed into the chamber from the magazine.

b. Semi-automatic handguns are further divided into single action, double action and double action only. In single action and double action, the hammer stays cocked after each shot is fired. In double action only, the hammer returns to the forward position after each shot is fired.

c. Semi-automatic safeties vary considerably. Most are located near the hammer. Check your owner's manual or consult with a qualified gunsmith.

Figure 34. Single action semi-automatic handgun

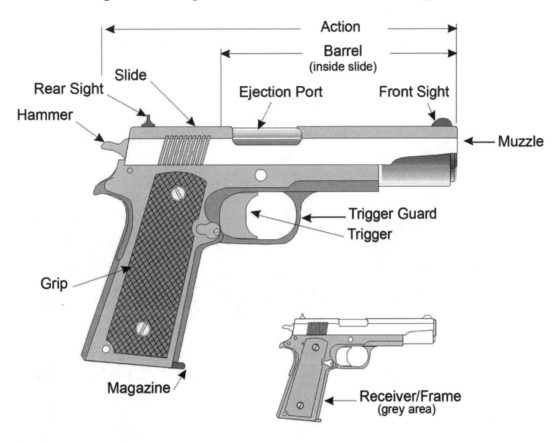

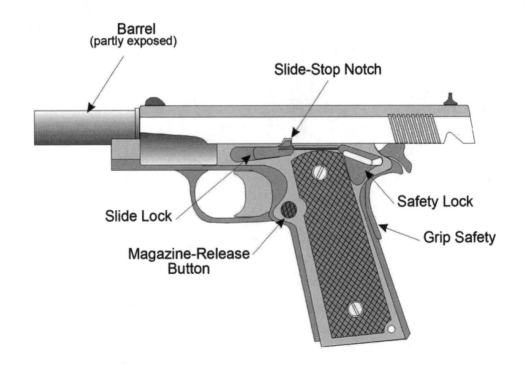

Figure 35. Double action semi-automatic handgun

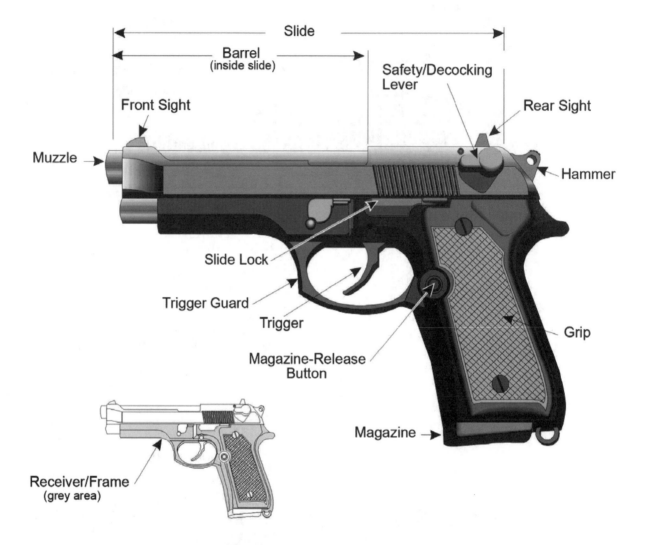

4.10.1 Single Action, Double Action, Double Action Only: Semi-Automatic / Unloading Procedure - PROVE it Safe

 Before attempting to unload a firearm, follow the Vital Four ACTS.

1. **P**oint the firearm in the safest available direction throughout the unloading procedure:

   - Make sure that nothing touches the trigger throughout this procedure.

   - Put the safety **ON**, if applicable, if it can be left on during the unloading process.

2. **R**emove all ammunition as follows:

   - Push the magazine-release button (see Figure 36) to remove the magazine (the source of all the ammunition except for possibly one chambered cartridge).

   - Pull the slide to the rear by doing the following:

     - Hold the handgun in the strong hand and point in a safe direction. Extend arm, locking wrist and elbow.

     - Pinch the rear of the slide with the weak hand. Ensure your hand does not cover the ejection port.

     - Pull the slide quickly and completely to the rear. This will extract and eject any cartridge or casing from the chamber.

     - Let any cartridge or casing fall on the shooting bench or range floor and leave it there until you have completed all the steps.

   - Lock the slide to the rear, normally by inserting the slide lock into the slide stop notch, where possible (see Figure 37).

3. **O**bserve the chamber to confirm that there is no cartridge or empty casing.

4. **V**erify that the feeding path to make sure it is clear of ammunition, casings, or foreign objects. Make certain the magazine has been removed.

5. **E**xamine the bore for lubricant, rust, or other obstructions.

Figure 36. Removing the magazine from a semi-automatic

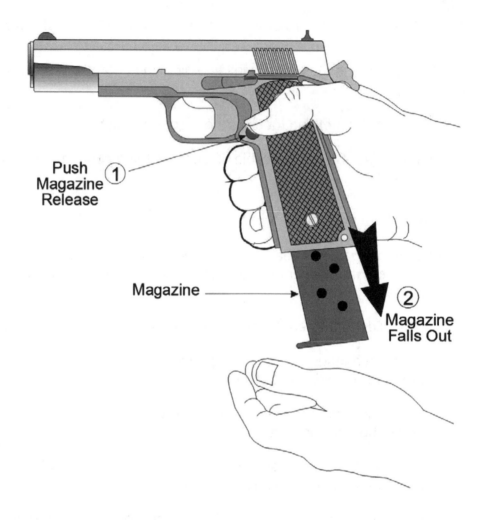

Figure 37. Locking the slide to the rear

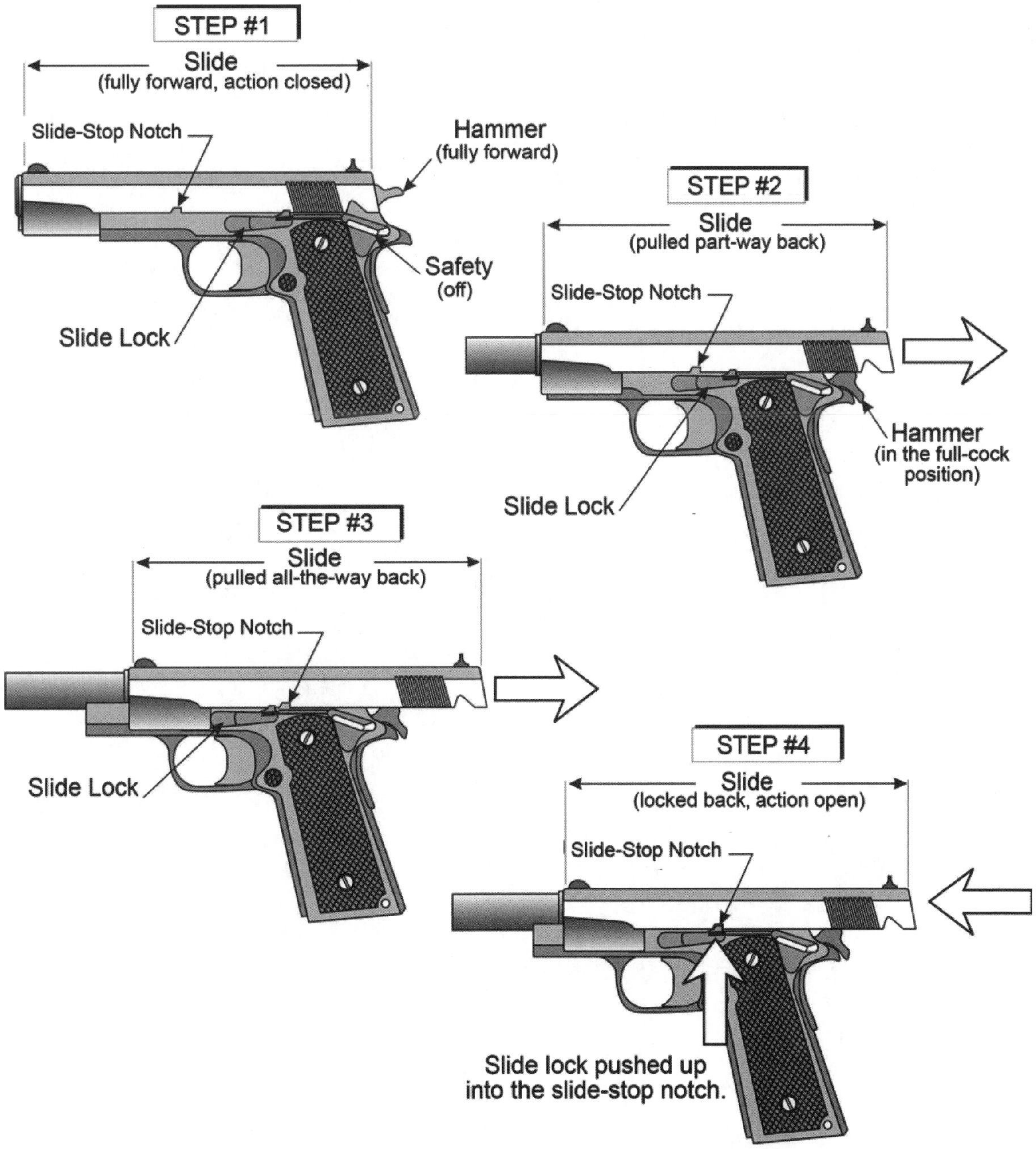

a. The firearm is now unloaded and safe until it leaves the direct control of the person who unloaded and **PROVEd** it safe.

b. Depending on make and model, magazine releases are located in different places such as the following:

- On the grip behind the trigger (as illustrated)

- At the bottom of the grip (front or rear)

- Some other location

See the owner's manual.

4.10.2 Single Action, Double Action, Double Action Only: Semi-Automatic / Loading Procedure

Only load a firearm when you intend to use it, and only in an area where it can be safely and legally discharged.

1. Prepare the firearm for loading by going through the complete unloading procedure - **PROVE** it safe.

2. Clear any obstructions from the chamber or barrel. Clean if required.

3. Point the firearm in the safest available direction throughout the loading and chambering procedure.

4. Make sure that nothing touches the trigger throughout this process.

5. Put the safety **ON**, if applicable, if it can be left on during the loading process.

6. Where possible, with the action open, select the correct ammunition by verifying that the data stamp on the firearm matches the head stamp on the cartridge.

7. Put the firearm down with the muzzle pointed in a safe direction and the action open, if possible. Charge the magazine by inserting cartridges into it.

8. Load the firearm by inserting the charged magazine into the magazine well with a firm push until it locks into the firearm (see Figure 38).

9. To chamber a cartridge:

    - Hold the handgun in the strong hand and point down range. Extend arm, locking wrist and elbow;

    - Pinch the rear of the slide with the weak hand. Ensure your hand does not cover the ejection port; and

    - Pull the slide quickly and completely to the rear and allow the slide to slip through your grip at the end of the stroke. The slide will be pushed forward by the recoil spring, chambering a cartridge.

10. Leave the safety on, if applicable, until ready to fire. In the case of the double action semi-automatic, activate the decocking lever.

The firearm is now loaded with a charged magazine and a chambered round, ready for use. It requires continuous care and attention until it is unloaded.

 Always be sure of your target and beyond.

Figure 38. Inserting a magazine to load a semi-automatic

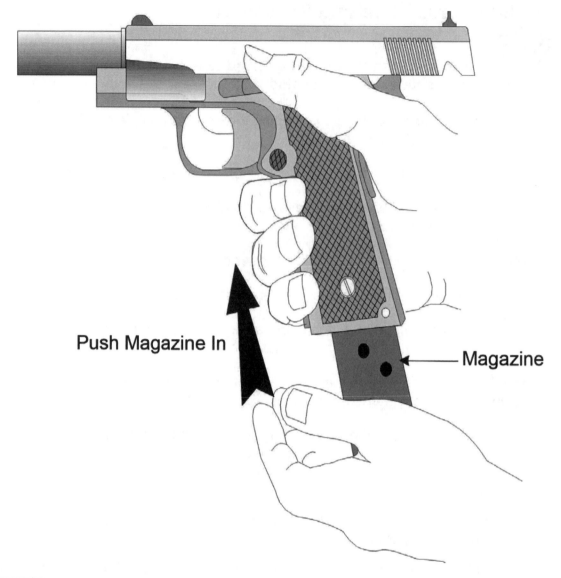

Push Magazine In

Magazine

 Magazine Size Limits:

Part 4 of the *Regulations Prescribing Certain Firearms and Other Weapons, Components, and Parts of Weapons, Accessories, Cartridge Magazines, Ammunition and Projectiles as Prohibited or Restricted* sets out the limit for the number of cartridges permitted for different types of magazines. Here are some examples:

- Uzi and Ingram type pistols (5-shot magazines); and
- Handguns (10-shot magazines).

For further information, refer to the *Regulations.*

Prior to July 1993, owners of large capacity cartridge magazines that were affected by the limits were able to retain them if they had been properly modified to comply with the limits.

4.11 Jammed Cartridges

a. Generally, using commercially made ammunition and a properly maintained firearm, malfunctions will not occur. Firearms jammed with a cartridge in the chamber(s) can be hazardous. This hazard, if not dealt with properly, may result in a serious accident. Consult a qualified person or gunsmith for information on how to perform this function in the safest possible manner with your particular firearm.

4.12 Review Questions

1. How should you examine the bore for obstructions?

    Using the rod

2. Can the presence of a half-cock notch on a firearm provide an additional safety? Why or why not?

    yes

3. Describe each of the Vital Four ACTS of firearms safety.

4. What does PROVE stand for? When is it used?

NOTES:

Section 5

FIRING TECHNIQUES

AND PROCEDURES

FOR HANDGUNS

5 - FIRING TECHNIQUES AND PROCEDURES FOR HANDGUNS

5.1 Personal Safety Protection

5.1.0 Overview

a. Like many active sports, shooting has the potential to cause personal injury. The careful shooter takes steps to avoid these injuries by wearing personal safety protection.

5.1.1 Eye Protection

a. There is a risk of eye injury in shooting. This can come from ejected cartridge casings. It can also come from fragments and other debris ejected during firing.

b. To avoid these hazards, shooters should wear safety glasses made of impact resistant glass or polycarbonate plastic with side shields. They also guard against firearm malfunctions or bullet fragments.

5.1.2 Hearing Protection

a. Continued unprotected exposure to shooting noise will cause hearing loss. The noise level of a gunshot is similar to that of a jet engine taking off at close range. The need for hearing protection is obvious.

b. Several types of hearing protection are available. On the firing range, shooters should always wear headphone-type hearing protectors. These protectors provide reasonable sound protection. They can also be used for years with minimum maintenance.

c. Earplugs are available in several types. Disposable earplugs are made of foam or wax, but they can only be used once.

d. There are also reusable earplugs made of rubber available in several sizes. They require care and cleaning after use.

e. For maximum hearing protection, it is highly recommended that both earplugs and headphone-type hearing protectors be worn.

5.1.3 Slips and Falls

a. Slips and falls may occur when handling firearms. This can best be avoided by using common sense.

b. If you do fall, remember your first action should be to control the muzzle of the firearm. This will prevent injury from an accidental discharge. The damage from a fall is probably less than the possible damage from an accidental shot.

c. Beware of cumbersome clothing. It can also interfere with the safe handling of your firearm.

Occasionally, a hot, ejected cartridge casing may come in contact with unprotected skin. This can cause a shooter to flinch. The sudden movement could result in unsafe muzzle control or accidental discharge. Therefore, button up the collar and sleeves of your shirt or blouse. This way, a hot cartridge casing cannot get inside.

5.2 Introduction to Marksmanship

a. Marksmanship is the ability to hit your mark or target. Good marksmanship is important for safe shooting.

b. Marksmanship depends on many factors including grip, shooting position, aim, trigger control, controlled breathing, and follow-through. These points are discussed in the following pages.

5.3 Shooting Positions

5.3.0 Overview

a. The correct firm grip gives you complete control of your handgun when it fires. Changing your grip will affect sight alignment and bullet placement on the target.

b. You can fire handguns either two-handed or one-handed and from several positions. Only the basic standing positions are described below.

5.3.1 The Two-Handed Grip

a. A similar two-handed grip is used for both revolvers and semi-automatics. Point the muzzle down range with your finger off the trigger and out of the trigger guard, until the sights are on the target. Grip the firearm as shown in the diagram using about the same pressure as you would to hold a carpenter's hammer (see Figure 39).

Figure 39. Two-handed grip for revolvers

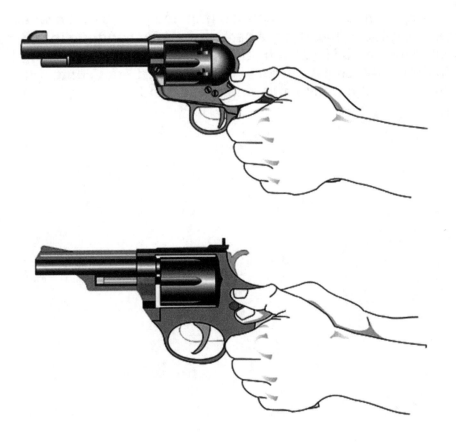

Figure 40. Two-handed grip for semi-automatics

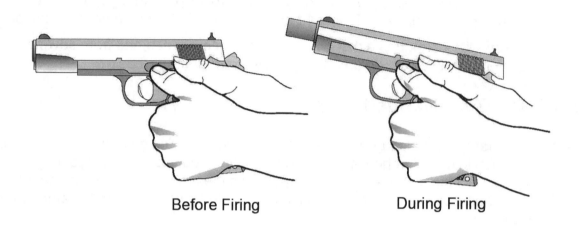

Before Firing   During Firing

Using an incorrect two-handed grip, the thumb of the weak hand may be behind the slide. While firing a semi-automatic handgun in this manner, your weak hand can be injured by the recoiling slide. When using the grip shown in Figure 40, be certain that your thumbs do not contact the slide and are positioned on the weak-hand side of the handgun.

5.3.2 The Two-Handed Stance

a. Stand with your body facing the target squarely. Spread your feet about shoulder width apart with weight distributed evenly on both feet to give you solid balance. Keep your knees straight but not locked (see Figure 41).

b. Stretch out both arms towards the target and lock your elbows. Keep your head up. Control your breathing.

Figure 41. Two-handed stance

5.3.3 The One-Handed Grip

 Hold firearm firmly when firing with one hand to avoid losing control.

a. Point the muzzle in a safe direction with your finger off the trigger. Wrap your fingers around the grip of the firearm with your thumb resting above the tips of your fingers as shown in the diagram (see Figure 42) Hold firmly but not too tightly, using about the same pressure as you would to hold a carpenter's hammer.

Figure 42. One-handed grip

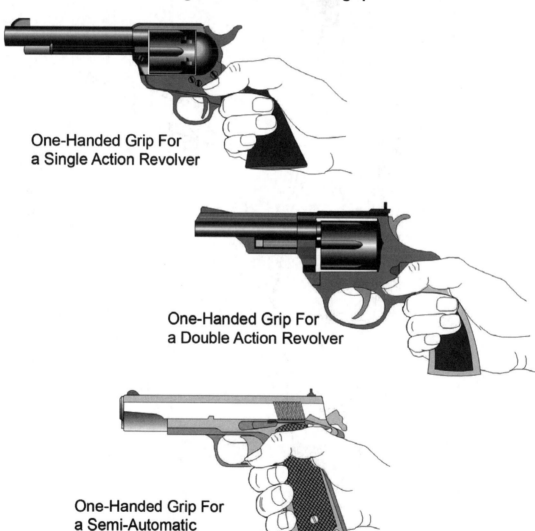

One-Handed Grip For
a Single Action Revolver

One-Handed Grip For
a Double Action Revolver

One-Handed Grip For
a Semi-Automatic

5.3.4 The One-Handed Stance

a. Stand with your body turned approximately 45 degrees from the target. Spread your feet about shoulder-width apart with weight distributed evenly on both feet to give you solid balance (see Figure 43). Keep your knees straight but not locked.

b. Keep the muzzle pointed down range and the barrel parallel to the ground. Stretch out your firing arm towards the target. Lock your elbow and wrist. Keep your head up. Control your breathing.

c. Always anchor your free hand to give stability when firing and to reduce body movement.

Figure 43. One-handed stance

5.4 Aiming Handguns

a. Use your master eye for sighting. It is the stronger of your two eyes and will judge speed, range and focus more accurately.

b. To find out which is your master eye, point your finger at a distant object with both eyes open. First close one eye and then the other. Your finger will remain lined up with the object when your master eye is open. Always try to aim with both eyes open as this gives a better view of the area surrounding the target.

c. You must also learn to correctly use your firearm's sight if your aim is to be accurate. Open sights require you to physically line up both rear and front sights with the target. This process is called sight alignment. When you aim any sight at a target, a sight picture is created (see Figure 44).

d. Scope and electronic red dot sights do not require conscious alignment (see Figure 45). Scope sights also have the advantage of magnifying your view of the target.

e. When preparing to aim through a scope or electronic red dot sight, do not look away from the target and then try to find the target again by looking through the scope. Instead, while steadily watching the target, raise the handgun correctly to the two-handed stance with arms fully extended. Point the firearm toward the target area until the sight comes up naturally between your eye and the target.

Figure 44. Open sights aligned on a target

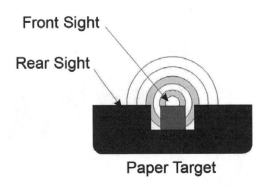

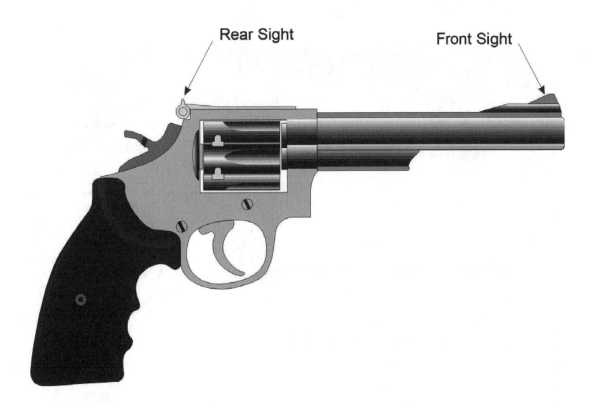

Figure 45. Types of sights aligned on targets

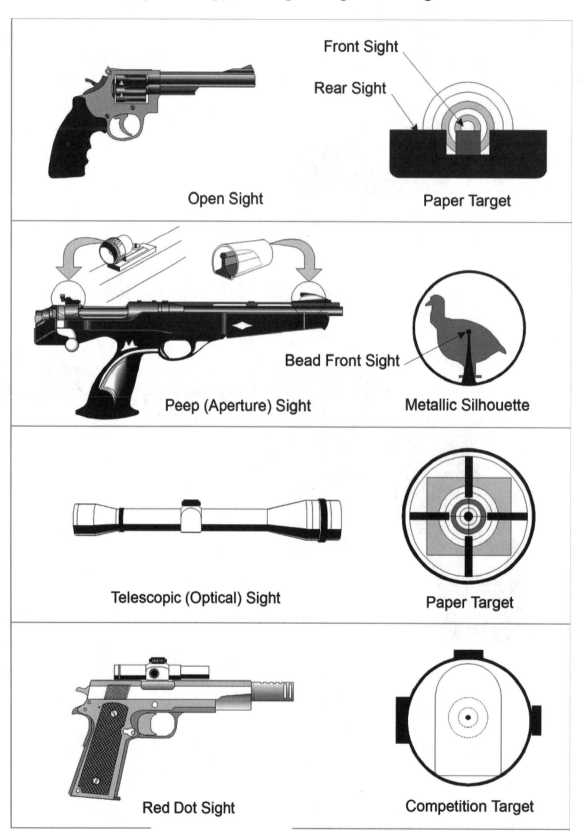

Front Sight

Rear Sight

Open Sight

Paper Target

Peep (Aperture) Sight

Bead Front Sight

Metallic Silhouette

Telescopic (Optical) Sight

Paper Target

Red Dot Sight

Competition Target

5.5 Trigger Control

a. Trigger control is essential for accurate shooting. When the sights are aligned on the target, squeeze the trigger slowly and steadily. Avoid yanking or pulling. Anything other than a smooth squeeze will cause the firearm to move and send the shot off target.

b. Don't anticipate the shot.

5.6 Controlled Breathing

a. You need to control your breathing to shoot accurately. The firearm barrel will move unless you control your breathing when you fire.

b. When you are in shooting position, take a few deep breaths. Exhale a portion of the last one. Hold your breath while you aim and then squeeze the trigger. This will help you keep the sights on the target.

c. If you hold your breath too long (more than about 8 seconds), you may lose your concentration and miss the target. If you run out of breath before firing, take another breath and re-aim.

5.7 Follow-Through

a. Follow-through simply means maintaining your sight picture and/or shooting position, after discharging the firearm. If you do not follow through, it is more likely that your shot will be off target.

5.8 Safety Procedures at the Range

5.8.1 Range Safety Rules

a. Every range has rules of safe behaviour. These may vary but will normally include the standard ones shown below:

1. The muzzle must always be pointed down range.

2. The action of any firearm must be open at all times except when actually shooting.

3. Firearms must be handled, loaded and discharged ONLY at the firing line.

4. No firearm is loaded until the command to load is given by the range officer.

5. Fingers must be kept out of the trigger guard and off the trigger until the firearm is pointed down range.

6. Upon the command "cease-fire," all firing stops **at once**. Firearms are unloaded. Actions are opened. Firearms are laid on the mat or on the table. Their muzzles point in a safe direction down range. The shooter steps back from the firing line, behind the cease-fire line.

7. The range officer will inspect each firearm before allowing anyone to go forward of the firing line.

8. During a cease-fire, no one will handle firearms or ammunition or return to the firing line. At this point, wait for further range commands before any further activity. Persons not engaged in changing targets down range should stand well behind the cease-fire line (see Figure 46).

9. Use hearing and eye protection.

 In an emergency, anyone can call a cease-fire.

Figure 46. Range layout

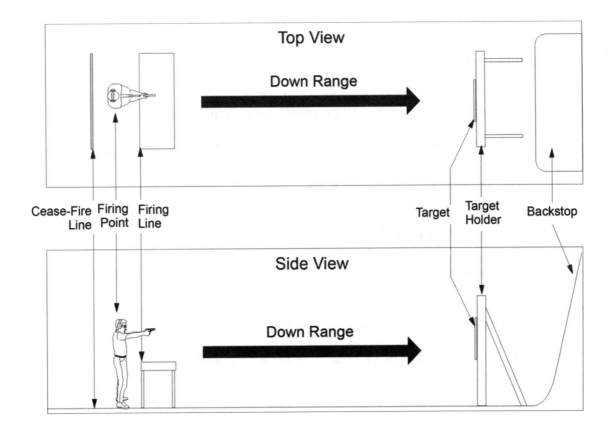

b. In addition to the above rules, below are several others we recommend you follow:

Additional Range Safety Suggestions

1. Minors and guests should be under direct supervision at all times while shooting.

2. When dealing with minors, all ammunition should be under the control of the immediate supervisor or the range officer. Check with your range for any further restrictions.

3. Firearms should be checked by the range officer on the cease-fire. This is to be sure that all actions are opened and no cartridges are in the breech.

4. Unloaded firearms not in use are to be placed on the bench or table with the action open or kept in a case. They should be moved with the muzzle pointed in the safest available direction or cased at the firing line.

5. Never allow horseplay, careless handling of firearms or any other distraction while shooting is in progress.

6. Make sure you are using the correct ammunition for your firearm and as approved by the range.

7. Never shoot at target holders or other range equipment.

8. Do not discharge firearms outside of designated range property or posted range use times.

5.8.2 Range Courtesy

a. There are also certain standards of range courtesy. Considerate shooters follow them. Some of these standards are listed below:

1. Rules and procedures vary between ranges. Check and obey local rules. There should be a safety briefing before starting.

2. Sign in to the firing range upon arrival.

3. Avoid interrupting or distracting others when they are shooting.

4. Do not smoke on the firing line.

5. Ask the owner's or shooter's permission before handling that person's firearm or equipment.

6. Leave enough space between you and others to ensure safety.

7. If firing particularly smoky firearms, shoot from downwind of other shooters on the firing line. Black powder firearms are especially smoky.

8. Do not fire on other people's targets, targets not directly downrange from yourself, or any target that may disturb others.

9. Those firing semi-automatic firearms should take a firing point where other people will not be disturbed by ejected casings.

10. Rapid firing may disturb those sighting-in or doing deliberate target work.

11. Clean up after shooting. Pick up cartridge casings. Take down targets.

12. Put away any range-owned equipment you have used. For example, sandbags or bench rests.

5.8.3 Range Commands

a. The following are examples of typical range commands:

- "The range is active."

- "Cease-fire."

- "The range is no longer active."

Range commands and signals vary between shooting sports, ranges and jurisdictions. Be sure you are aware of and clearly understand the commands and signals used in your area. If you are unsure, ask the Range Officer or a local official before you go to the range (see Appendix H: Visual Range Signals and Devices).

5.9 Targets

5.9.1 Acceptable Targets

a. Before firing at any target, verify the target by asking yourself the following questions:

1. Am I sure of the identity of my target?

2. Can I see it clearly?

3. Am I positive it is exactly the target I want?

4. Is it a permitted target?

5. Is it the proper target at a shooting range?

6. Is anything else in the line of fire, either in front or beside or behind the target?

7. Could anything else come suddenly into the line of fire?

5.9.2 Unacceptable Targets

a. Below are examples of unacceptable targets:

   1. Any target which, when fired upon, may damage the range. These include signs and main target holder supports;

   2. Someone else's target on the range;

   3. Any target which is not directly in front of your firing point at the firing line;

   4. Any target which, when fired upon, may disturb others. For example: discharging firearms outside of posted range use times;

   5. Any target or a material or shape that can cause ricochets such as target holder frames or concrete walkways; and

   6. Any target made of glass or other material that causes fragment hazards.

 Hunting with a handgun is not permitted in Canada.

5.10 Review Questions

1. Describe what you do after a cease-fire is called.

   Act &Proate, Step away

2. Describe the two shooting positions for handguns.

   One & two handed stand al

3. Name five examples of unacceptable targets.

   - Someone else's target
   - any target not infront of you
   - target that cauke ricochet
   - any target to damage the range.

NOTES:

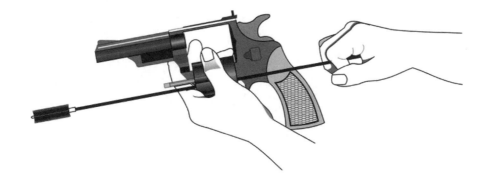

Section 6

CARE OF

RESTRICTED FIREARMS

6 - CARE OF RESTRICTED FIREARMS

6.1 Firearm Servicing

⚠ Ensure that all firearms are unloaded and PROVEd safe before attempting to clean. Refer to Section 4 on unloading procedures - PROVE.

a. Always be sure your firearm is functioning properly. A firearm that does not work properly is an unsafe firearm.

b. This section on minor maintenance and servicing procedures for your firearm is included for general information only. Specific information on cleaning and servicing your firearm is available in your firearm owner's manual, at a gun shop, or from a gunsmith. Accidents can occur if these procedures are not performed correctly.

c. Firearms are precision instruments. Even minor repairs should be made by qualified individuals. **Unqualified persons should never try to repair or modify any firearm**.

d. The average user should do basic cleaning and lubrication only.

Example of an accident

Someone was preparing to clean a loaded firearm with the action closed, and dropped it. The rifle fired when it hit the floor. Someone in the next room was killed.

The contributing factors were as follows:

- Having a loaded firearm in a house
- Lack of muzzle control
- Failing to PROVE the firearm unloaded
- Action was closed

6.2 Firearm Cleaning

6.2.0 Overview

a. Information on cleaning firearms safely may be obtained from your firearm owner's manual. If you do not have one, contact the manufacturer. Accidents can happen if the cleaning procedure is not performed correctly.

b. Two major threats to firearm safety are as follows:

 1. Rust caused by moisture and condensation; and

 2. Excessive build-up of residue or rust in the firearm.

c. Either may cause excessive pressure, damaging the barrel. This is why regular cleaning is recommended.

d. The barrel of a firearm should be cleaned after every use. This will protect its finish. It will also help keep it in good working order. For instructions on cleaning the rest of the firearm, check your owner's manual.

e. Modern smokeless primers and powders are non-corrosive. However, some older military surplus ammunition still contains corrosive chemicals. If you use corrosive ammunition, you should clean your firearm immediately after you use it.

f. Any firearm that has been stored for a long time must be cleaned thoroughly before use. Cleaning before using is required when the firearm has been exposed to moisture or dirt.

If cleaning your firearm requires disassembly, consult your owner's manual. If disassembly is required to clean a firearm, always wear safety glasses. Oil or moisture can be very dangerous in cold weather. They may cause safeties and other firing mechanism parts to freeze in a firing position. Later, when the firearm thaws, it may fire. Residue or rust in the chamber or barrel may cause serious pressure build-up. Also, oil may mix with unburnt powder and other dirt causing the firearm to jam.

6.2.1 Cleaning Materials

a. To clean a firearm properly, you need the following materials:

   - A cleaning rod and attachments (be sure to use the right size for the firearm), such as a bore brush

   - Tips to hold cloth patches

   - Patches

   - Powder solvent (also called "bore cleaner")

   - Light gun oil

   - A soft cloth

b. If possible, clean your firearm from the breech toward the muzzle. Avoid cleaning from the muzzle toward the breech.

c. However, you may have to clean some types from the muzzle end. In this case, lock the breech open. This permits the passage of the cleaning rod completely through the barrel. You will find a pull-through cleaning device helpful. Avoid rubbing the cleaning rod on the muzzle. Damage to the crown at the muzzle may occur. It is beneficial to insert a cloth into the open action to collect residue, to prevent dirt from entering the action, and to prevent damage to the firearm.

d. When cleaning a bolt action, remove the bolt, if possible. Clean the firearm from the breech end. Some firearms are easier to clean if you remove the barrel first.

While cleaning a firearm, remember and follow the Vital Four ACTS. These additional recommended practices for home safety with firearms might prevent accidents:

1. **Make sure no ammunition is nearby during cleaning.**

2. **Never allow a loaded firearm in any building or living area.**

3. **Always give cleaning your firearm your full attention. Never clean a firearm while doing something else, like watching television.**

6.2.2 General Cleaning Procedures

1. Attach the bore brush to the cleaning rod. Apply bore cleaner to the brush.

2. Run the brush through the bore of the barrel/chamber(s) several times. Be sure that the brush sticks out completely. Then, draw it back through the barrel (see Figure 47).

   NOTE: When cleaning a revolver, always support the cylinder to avoid potential damage.

3. Remove the bore brush from the cleaning rod. Attach a patch-holder tip and a proper size cloth patch. Pour solvent on the cloth patch. Run it through the bore of the barrel/chamber(s) several times. Remove the cloth patch from the rod tip.

4. Next, run a clean, dry patch through the bore/chamber(s) several times.

5. If the patch comes out dirty, repeat the first four steps. Do this until a patch finally comes through clean.

6. Next, run a lightly oiled patch through the bore/chamber(s). Use only light gun oil.

7. Wipe the outside of the firearm with a clean cloth and apply a light coat of gun oil or rust preventative to the metal surfaces. You should also maintain the condition of the stock by applying the appropriate wood treatment (see the owner's manual).

8. Always store your firearm properly.

9. Remember, before the next firing of the firearm, run a dry patch through the bore and the chamber(s) to remove any oil.

Figure 47. Cleaning a double action revolver cylinder from the breech to the muzzle

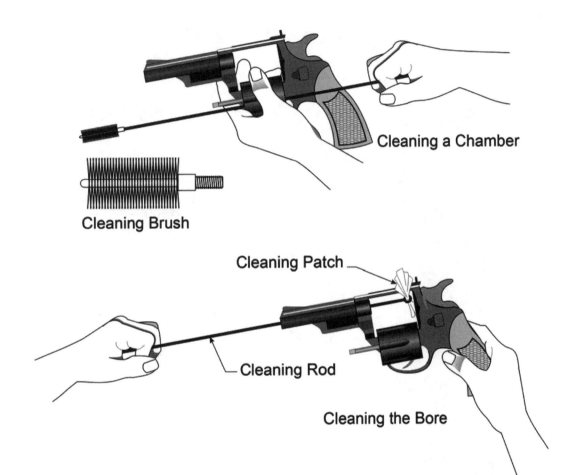

Cleaning a Chamber

Cleaning Brush

Cleaning Patch

Cleaning Rod

Cleaning the Bore

After cleaning a firearm for storage, avoid skin contact with metal parts. Acids in perspiration can cause rust.

Figure 48. Cleaning a semi-automatic handgun

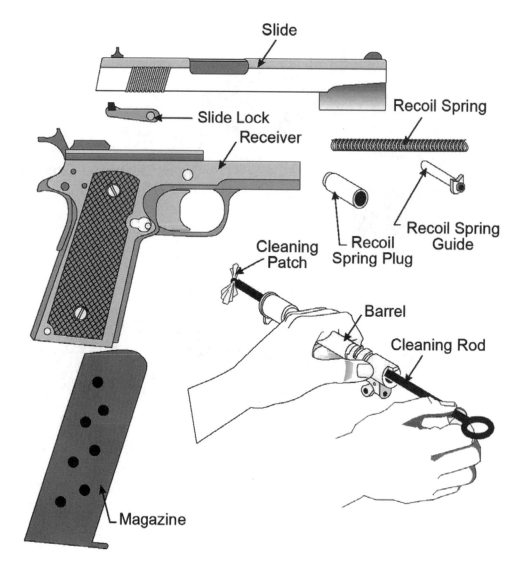

6.2.3 Cleaning a Muzzleloader

a. A black powder firearm must be properly cleaned after every firing session. Black powder is very corrosive. It attracts moisture, which causes rust.

b. Cleaning black powder firearms improperly can result in carbon build-up in the barrel, which may cause coking. This condition may cause a glowing ember to remain after firing, resulting in a dangerous situation if the firearm is reloaded.

It is strongly recommended that persons interested in muzzleloading seek additional training from experienced individuals.

c. Use either commercial black powder cleaning solvent or hot, soapy water.

d. You will also need a ramrod with a cleaning patch attached. Use a rod as close to the bore diameter as possible. Refer to the owner's manual.

e. Use wet patches to soften the dried powder.

   1. Detach the barrel and place the lock end in a container of soapy water.

   2. Attach a patch to the ramrod. Insert the ramrod into the barrel. Pump the ramrod up and down until water flows from the top end of the barrel.

   3. Repeat step 2. Change the water as it becomes dirty. Repeat until the water stays clean.

   4. Dry the barrel out with several dry patches. Oil thoroughly with good gun oil.

   5. Remove the lock for cleaning and oiling after every use.

f. If cleaning a black powder revolver, follow the manufacturer's instructions for the proper cleaning methods.

6.2.4 Cleaning Ammunition

a. Ammunition should also be kept clean and dry. Oil, sand or dirt on the cartridge can damage the firearm. It could also cause jamming of the action.

b. Avoid exposing your ammunition to heat and vibration. Powder can decay and become unpredictable if exposed to excessive heat and long-term vibration.

Primers are adversely affected by exposure to penetrating oils. Do not clean your ammunition with an oily rag. Before using any firearm, remove oil or grease from inside the barrel. Increased pressure caused by dirt or oil may cause the barrel to burst. This comes from the pressure generated in a dirty barrel when a bullet is fired through it. After storage and before you use the firearm again, run a clean patch through the bore. Remove all grease and oil. Always ensure your firearm is in good working order. Ensure that you have followed the Vital Four ACTS in order to PROVE the firearm safe before attempting to clean and throughout the entire cleaning procedure.

6.3 Review Questions

1. What procedure should you follow to clean a black powder muzzleloader?

    Act & Proove ...or Soapy water   Pg. 195

2. What is the first step to take when preparing to clean a firearm?

    no distraction ; Act & Proove

3. Why should oil or grease be removed from inside the barrel of a firearm?

    damage.

NOTES:

Section 7

SOCIAL RESPONSIBILITIES OF

THE FIREARMS OWNER/USER

7 - SOCIAL RESPONSIBILITIES OF THE FIREARMS OWNER/USER

7.1 Firearm-Related Deaths and Injuries

a. The main purpose of this course is to promote the safe use and handling of firearms. Increased safety awareness will help prevent both the accidental and deliberate misuse of firearms.

b. Most safety courses concentrate on the prevention of accidents caused by careless use or unintentional discharge of firearms. However, the intentional misuse of firearms in suicides and homicides results in far more deaths and serious injuries.

c. Suicides and homicides are often acts of sudden impulse. Many of them might not have happened if the firearms and ammunition were stored safely. For this reason, this course stresses the safe handling and use of restricted firearms and ammunition, and their secure storage.

d. The intentional misuse of firearms, resulting in suicide and homicide, has fallen since the eighties. Unintentional misuse of firearms, resulting in accidents, has also fallen.

7.2 Intentional Misuse of Firearms

7.2.0 Overview

a. The misuse of firearms can lead to tragic results. Firearms are not unique that way. This is also true of automobiles, power tools, and even kitchen knives.

7.2.1 Suicide

a. In Canada, the great majority of firearm-related deaths are suicides. In many cases, suicide is an act of sudden impulse. It is often brought on by some temporary setback or moment of depression. These occurrences may seem trivial to the outside observer. They are not trivial to the person experiencing them. Even a failed exam, an argument with a girlfriend or boyfriend, or an accident with the family car can bring it on.

Examples of Suicide and Attempted Suicide

1. A young man of 18 had an accident with his father's truck. When he got home, the father scolded him. The father then left to examine the truck at the repair shop. The young man got his father's firearm that was kept unsecured at home. He loaded a cartridge into it and shot himself. This was not the first time he had tried suicide. But this time he succeeded.

2. A young man broke up with his girlfriend. He went home where a firearm and ammunition were kept in an unlocked closet. He shot himself in the face. Surgery saved his life but he lost an eye. He says that if no firearm had been readily available, he would not have attempted suicide. That was twenty years ago. He has not tried again.

The contributing factors were as follows:

- Firearm not locked or stored securely

- Ammunition not stored properly

 One line of defense against suicide is delayed access to firearms.

b. Many people think that a person trying to commit suicide will just find another method if a firearm is not available. Studies show that this is not always true. If a weapon cannot be found right away, some individuals considering suicide give the idea up and never try again.

c. Even if another method is used, it may not be as lethal as a firearm. Those people who survive a suicide attempt, quite often do not try again. In fact, a few weeks later, many survivors are pleased they were not successful. With a firearm, a suicidal person often does not get a second chance.

7.2.2 Homicide

a. Homicide means causing the death of another human being. In Canada, firearms-related homicides are the second highest cause of firearms related death.

b. Like suicides, there are common misunderstandings about homicides. For example, a significant number of homicides are carried out by people with no criminal record.

c. If a firearm is available in these situations, it is more likely to be used. If not a firearm, another weapon may be used in the heat of the moment, like a fist, a club or a knife. But the chances of killing someone with them are lower than with a firearm.

d. Many suicides and homicides are acts of sudden, temporary impulse. The majority are carried out by people in their own homes while under great strain. Often, alcohol or drug abuse is also involved.

Example of Homicide

A husband and wife were in the process of separating. He was unemployed; she was not. Family, friends and neighbours knew they were having violent disputes. The police did not. Shortly after the husband became aware that his wife wanted to confirm their permanent separation, and after he was informed that she was involved with another man, he took a shotgun and killed her. He was under the influence of alcohol.

The contributing factors were as follows:

- Easy access to firearms and ammunition

- Alcohol

- No alternate storage of firearms used

---

e. What can the average firearm owner do about this? Impulse and availability of firearms and ammunition are two factors. If there is no easy access, the impulse to act in a violent way often weakens in a few minutes or hours.

Be sure your firearms and ammunition are properly stored. Make them difficult to get at. Store each away separately and locked securely.

7.2.3 Signs of Risk

a. As noted in the previous examples, sometimes it is possible to detect the signs that someone may be at risk of committing suicide or homicide. You can sometimes anticipate violent situations before they happen. Remember, these events can happen in our own homes or those of friends or neighbours.

b. When these situations seem to be developing, it is good practice to remove all firearms. This is true even if they are properly stored. Consider storing the firearms at an alternate location, and, if necessary, notify the police of the situation.

Example of Storing Firearms at an Alternate Location

A ten-year-old boy died suddenly of an accident at home. The parents were very upset, and the police who were at the scene asked if firearms were present in the household. When the father said that he owned three firearms, the police requested permission to take the firearms and store them at the police station for a few days. The father agreed. He picked up his firearms one week later, and he agreed with police that persons who face such a tragedy could be tempted to harm themselves or others.

The contributing factor was as follows:
*   Removal of firearms in a stressful situation

---

c. You would not hesitate to prevent a friend or relative from drinking and driving. Do not hesitate to prevent the misuse of firearms by others.

7.3 Firearms Reported Lost, Missing or Stolen

a. Owners of restricted or prohibited firearms were required under the former *Criminal Code* to report the loss or theft of their restricted or prohibited firearms because it was only these that had to be registered. Because the *Firearms Act* now extends registration to all firearms, the requirement to report a loss or theft is also extended to non-restricted firearms. A person failing to report a firearm lost, missing or stolen to a peace officer, firearms officer, or chief firearms officer may be fined and/or jailed. The high number of firearms reported lost, missing or stolen each year may contribute to the intentional misuse of firearms. For further information on this subject, see Appendix G: Reporting Lost of Stolen Firearms, etc. at the back of this handbook or section 105 of Part III of the *Criminal Code*.

Example of an Accident Where Stolen Firearms Were Not Reported

A 15-year-old boy stole six firearms from a man's house. Out of fear, the man did not immediately report his firearms missing because they were improperly stored in a closet without a secure locking device. The next day, at the time of reporting, he was unaware that, only four hours earlier, the 15-year-old boy had loaded one of his firearms, pointed the firearm at himself in jest, discharged the firearm, and killed himself. Three of the firearms remain missing, and police fear that they are on the street.

The contributing factors were as follows:

- Firearms not locked or stored securely
- Failure to immediately report the loss of firearms
- Careless handling of a firearm

7.4 Secure Storage

a. Secure firearm storage is the best way to limit theft and deliberate misuse of firearms. It should not be easy for unauthorized users to get firearms and ammunition.

b. Do not leave the key or combination to the firearm storage area or container lying around. Do not give them out to others. Also, do not let it become widely known that you have firearms.

c. Locking up firearms and ammunition is important and, in many cases, required by law.

 Carelessly stored firearms may be misused.

d. Make access to firearms and ammunition difficult. Many suicides and homicides arise from sudden impulses. If firearms and ammunition are difficult to get, there may be a delay in acting on the impulse to do harm. This delay may be enough to make the impulse decrease or go away.

e. Secure storage of firearms and ammunition may act as a deterrent to easy theft by criminals. Remember: you are responsible for your firearms 24 hours a day. This is both a legal and a moral responsibility. It is wise to store them safely and securely when you are not physically in control of them. This may cause some inconvenience, but it may also save a person from death or serious injury.

7.5 Unintentional Misuse of Firearms

a. Most firearm accidents happen because of one or more of the following reasons:

- Unauthorized access or improper storage

- Lack of control of muzzle direction

- Careless or ignorant use

- Accidental firing

- Users who are not qualified

- Aiming or firing at the wrong target

- Using the wrong ammunition

 Follow the Vital Four ACTS.

b. Improper storage of firearms may lead to tragedy, if firearms get into the hands of unqualified or unauthorized persons.

Examples of Accidents

1. A firearm had been left loaded and within easy reach. A child started playing with it. A parent grabbed the firearm by the barrel. He pulled it away from the child. It fired and the parent was wounded.

2. Two young children were playing in their home. They found a firearm in the bedroom closet. One was killed when the firearm discharged.

The contributing factors were as follows:

- Improper storage of a firearm

- Unsafe muzzle direction

- Failure to teach firearm awareness to family members

---

c. Most accidents involve a muzzle being pointed at the holder of the firearm or someone else. The firearm is accidentally fired, because of one of the following reasons:

-   Shooters have their finger in the trigger guard and on the trigger before they are absolutely ready to shoot, or

-   Some other object accidentally pushes on or presses the trigger.

d. Firearm accidents happen during loading and unloading.

Examples of Accidents

3. A man was loading his firearm with the muzzle pointing to his left. Another person was standing near by. The rifle accidentally fired and the other person was wounded.
4. Another young man was wounded when rushing to load a cartridge into his firearm. His finger was in the trigger guard and on the trigger.

The contributing factors were as follows:

-   Unsafe muzzle direction

-   Unsafe loading/unloading procedure

-   Finger in the trigger guard

---

e. Accidents can happen when the wrong ammunition is used.

Example of an Accident

5. A box of ammunition purchased at a store contained a similar but incorrect cartridge. A previous customer had probably switched it accidentally. When the firearm was fired, the barrel burst and injured the shooter's hands.

The contributing factors were as follows:

-   Failure to match the data stamp on the firearm with the head stamp on the cartridge

-   Carrying and using the wrong ammunition

7.6 Table 7 - Firearm Hazards and Precautions

Table 7. Firearm hazards and precautions

Firearm Hazards and Precautions	
Hazard	**Precautions**
Access by unqualified or unauthorized users	<ul><li>Disable action before storage or transport (or use trigger or cable lock)</li><li>Store firearms in a safely locked cabinet or container, out of view</li><li>Store ammunition separately and out of view</li><li>Supervise unqualified users</li></ul>
Accidental firing	<ul><li>Control muzzle direction at all times</li><li>Unload firearm when not in immediate use</li><li>Open action when handling</li><li>Keep finger off trigger and out of the trigger guard except when firing</li><li>Safety ON</li><li>No horseplay</li><li>A malfunctioning firearm may result in accidental discharge</li><li>Ensure your firearm is well maintained and regularly serviced</li></ul>
Wrong ammunition	<ul><li>Carry only correct ammunition</li><li>Check ammunition against firearm data stamp</li><li>Use proper ammunition for target and conditions</li><li>If re-loading, follow correct procedures</li><li>Improperly loaded ammunition can cause a firearm accident</li><li>Ensure you know how to load correctly</li></ul>
Ricochets	<ul><li>Be extra cautious when shooting at or towards flat or hard surfaces</li><li>Check area near or behind target before firing</li><li>Be extra cautious when shooting at or towards water</li></ul>
Wrong target	<ul><li>Identify target before firing</li><li>Know what is behind target</li><li>Make sure the backstop is adequate</li></ul>

7.7 Social Responsibilities and Ethics

a. As a firearms user, you have certain legal obligations to the community at large. In some cases, however, sticking to the letter of the law is not enough. The spirit of the law must also be followed. The welfare and well being of your fellow citizens must come first.

b. Below are some moral and social rules. They must be part of the code of ethics for anyone possessing firearms.

1. **Store all firearms and ammunition properly.** Keep your firearms and ammunition properly secured and out of sight.

2. **Explain firearms safety to all family members.** Everyone in a home where firearms are kept should know the safety rules. Firearms are no different than dangerous tools or poisons in the home. The proper use and handling of firearms and ammunition must be taught to the entire family. The key or combination number to secure locking devices should be kept away from and out of the reach of children and unauthorized adults.

3. **Remove firearms from situations of potential violence.** You may become aware of a situation where violence or tragedy could occur. In such cases, it is wise to go beyond the safe storage of firearms. Completely remove firearms that may be present. If this is not possible, at least notify the police of the situation.

4. **Act sensibly and carefully while around firearms**. Always pay close attention to what you and others around you are doing. Make sure that everyone is acting safely and responsibly.

5. **Never consume drugs or alcoholic beverages when around firearms.** Do not go shooting with anyone who has. Alcohol and drugs can affect your mental or physical reactions. Both prescription and non-prescription drugs can affect your alertness, senses and balance. Some types of allergy medicines are a good example. Always stay fully alert when around firearms.

6. **Always get permission before shooting on someone else's property.** Make sure you are welcome and permitted before you shoot anywhere. Do this whether the land belongs to the crown, to a local club, or a private citizen. Make sure that you can shoot there safely. For example, someone else may be shooting there at the same time.

7. **Have your eyesight checked regularly**. Shooting requires good vision for target identification and accuracy. Be sure of your target and beyond.

8. **Maintain your firearm in good working order.** If required, have a qualified person service your firearm.

9. **Avoid firing near any buildings or roads.** Respect the rights of others to safe travel and undisturbed use of their property. Only shoot near buildings with authorized permission, and only if it is legal and safe.

10. **Know and respect firearms regulations and local by-laws.** Some of these are listed in Section 7.8.

11. **Wear safety equipment.** Encourage others to do the same. Safety equipment may include, but should not be limited to, eye and hearing protection, gloves, caps, and proper clothing.

Table 8. Social responsibilities of a firearm user

Social Responsibilities of a Firearm User **(summary of)**
1. Store all firearms and ammunition properly.
2. Explain firearms safety to all family members.
3. Remove firearms from situations of potential violence.
4. Act sensibly and carefully while around firearms.
5. Never consume drugs or alcoholic beverages when around firearms.
6. Always get permission before shooting on someone else's property.
7. Have your eyesight checked regularly.
8. Maintain your firearm in good working order.
9. Avoid firing near any buildings or roads.
10. Know and respect firearms regulations and local by-laws.
11. Wear safety equipment.

7.8 Legal Responsibilities

a. As a firearm owner and user, you have legal as well as social responsibilities. These responsibilities are laid down in federal, provincial / territorial and municipal laws and regulations. Table 9 describes a few of the regulations that come from each level of government.

Table 9. Some legal responsibilities of a firearm user

SOME LEGAL RESPONSIBILITIES of a FIREARM USER	
Government Level	**Example of Law or Regulation**
Federal (e.g. *Firearms Act* and its *Regulations, Criminal Code*)	All firearm owners need a valid licence, and all firearms must be registered. If you are the holder of a valid Firearms Licence, you must inform the RCMP/CAFC when you change your address. Persons holding a valid Possession Only Licence (POL) may borrow the same class of firearms that he/she is licenced to own. Persons holding a valid Possession and Acquisition Licence may borrow, buy, inherit or otherwise acquire the same class of firearm that he/she is licenced to own.
Provincial/Territorial (e.g. *Game, Fish and Wildlife Acts*)	Some provinces/territories may require anyone who hunts with a non-restricted firearm to wear blaze orange clothing. Some restrict shooting across or within a certain distance of roads or dwellings. Some provincial/territorial laws may limit your use of motorized vehicles while hunting or shooting.
Municipal/County/Local (e.g. Noise, Nuisance, Zoning, By-laws)	Some municipalities or counties may not allow firing of a firearm under any circumstances within their boundaries. Some will regulate firing times and/or closeness to dwellings.

7.9 Other Duties of Firearm Owners/Users

a. Automobile drivers are expected to know the rules of the road. They are also required to know any driving related laws and regulations.

b. A firearm owner/user must also keep informed about the laws and regulations affecting the use of firearms and ammunition.

c. Going beyond what the regulations require will increase your safety. Some suggestions are listed below:

- Keep an inventory of your firearms. Also keep any supporting documents such as registration certificates, photographs and owner's manual. Store these documents in a safe place. This will help you describe any firearms that may be stolen or lost. It will also be easier for you to find your owner's manual and records of service or repair.

- Keep informed. Changes may occur in laws and regulations from time to time. This can happen at any level, whether at the federal, provincial/territorial or municipal.

- Avoid advertising about the firearms in your home. You may be inviting theft.

d. You can be prosecuted if you ignore regulations that apply to firearm owners and users.

Every person commits an offence who, without lawful excuse, points a firearm at another person, whether the firearm is loaded or unloaded, and is:

1. **guilty of an indictable offence and liable to imprisonment for a term not exceeding five years, or**

2. **guilty of an offence punishable on summary conviction (a fine of $2,000 and/or six months' imprisonment).**

Reference: Subsections 87(1) and (2) of Part III of the *Criminal Code*

Every person who stores, displays transports or handles any firearm in a manner contrary to the *Storage, Display, Transportation and Handling of Firearms by Individuals Regulations* is:

1. **guilty of an indictable offence and liable to imprisonment,**

    • **in the case of a first offence, for a term not exceeding two years, and**

    • **in the case of a second or subsequent offence, for a term not exceeding five years; or**

2. **guilty of an offence punishable on summary conviction (a fine of $2,000 and/or six months' imprisonment).**

Reference: Subsections 86(2) and (3) of Part III of the *Criminal Code*

e. Not all firearms laws can be included in this handbook. If you are in any doubt about the regulations or if you need more information, you can take the following steps:

    1. Contact a firearms officer.

    2. Obtain a copy of the federal legislation and regulations from your Chief Firearms Officer.

f. You can also get information about provincial/territorial and municipal laws and regulations from your local police station or wildlife agency.

7.10 Review Questions

1. Suicide and homicide are the leading causes of firearms-related deaths and injuries. How may this type of firearms misuse be reduced?

2. List three frequent contributing factors that may lead to firearm accidents.

3. List five examples of socially responsible behaviour for a firearms user.

NOTES:

Section 8

SAFE STORAGE, DISPLAY,

TRANSPORTATION AND HANDLING

OF RESTRICTED FIREARMS

8 - SAFE STORAGE, DISPLAY, TRANSPORTATION AND HANDLING OF RESTRICTED FIREARMS

8.1 Classes of Firearms

8.1.0 Overview

a. Table 10 in Section 8.1.1, Table 11 in Section 8.1.2 and Table 12 in Section 8.1.3 provide a brief description of each class of firearms. For legal references, however, please refer to the *Firearms Act* and its *Regulations*, and Part III of the *Criminal Code*.

8.1.1 Table 10 - Non-Restricted Firearms

Table 10. Non-restricted firearms

Non-Restricted Firearms
Generally, firearms commonly used for hunting or sporting purposes such as target shooting are included in this class. The following are examples of non-restricted firearms: • Rifles • Shotguns

8.1.2 Table 11 - Restricted Firearms

Table 11. Restricted firearms

Restricted Firearms
In general, individuals may possess restricted firearms for one or more of the following reasons: lawful profession or occupation, target practice or competition, as part of a gun collection or, in some rare cases, for the protection of life. The following are examples of restricted firearms: • A handgun which is not a prohibited firearm   • A firearm that is not a prohibited firearm, has a barrel less than 470 mm (18½ inches) in length, and discharges centre-fire ammunition in a semi-automatic manner   • A firearm that is designed or adapted to be fired when reduced to a length of less than 660 mm (26 inches) by folding, telescoping or otherwise   • A firearm of any kind that is prescribed by regulation to be a restricted firearm

It must be noted that some rifles and shotguns are considered restricted or prohibited. Persons wishing to acquire such firearms should contact a firearms officer for further information.

8.1.3 Table 12 - Prohibited Firearms

Table 12. Prohibited firearms

Prohibited Firearms
In general, individuals cannot acquire the types of firearms that fall into the prohibited class. Depending on the nature of their duties, employees of businesses and carriers, and public officers (police or peace officer, firearms officer, prescribed employee of a federal, provincial or municipal government) may possess prohibited firearms. The following are examples of prohibited firearms: • Handguns with a barrel length equal to or less than 105 mm (4⅛ inches) • Handguns designed or adapted to discharge a 25- or 32-calibre cartridge (any of the above-noted handguns are not prohibited firearms if they are used in competitions governed by the rules of the International Shooting Union and prescribed by regulation) • "Sawed-off" rifles or "sawed-off" shotguns less than 660 mm (26 inches) in length • "Sawed-off" rifles or "sawed-off" shotguns 660 mm (26 inches) or greater in length and have barrel lengths of less than 457 mm (18 inches) • An automatic firearm • Any firearm that is prescribed by regulation to be a prohibited firearm

8.2 Ammunition, Prohibited Ammunition and Prohibited Devices

8.2.0 Overview

a. Ammunition, prohibited ammunition and prohibited devices are defined in the Part III of the *Criminal Code*. The following tables provide a brief description of each group; see Table 13 below; see also Table 14 in Section 8.2.1 and Table 15 in Section 8.2.2. For a complete description, consult the *Criminal Code of Canada*.

Table 13. Ammunition

Ammunition
Ammunition is a cartridge containing a projectile that is designed to be discharged from a firearm. This includes caseless cartridges and shot shells.

8.2.1 Table 14 - Prohibited Ammunition

Table 14. Prohibited ammunition

Prohibited Ammunition
Individuals cannot acquire prohibited ammunition. Depending on the nature of their duties, employees of businesses and carriers, and public officers (police or peace officer, firearms officer, prescribed employee of a federal, provincial or municipal government) may possess prohibited ammunition. The following are examples of ammunition prescribed by regulation as prohibited ammunition: • Any cartridge that can be fired from a commonly available semi-automatic handgun or revolver and has a projectile specifically designed to penetrate body armour • Any projectile that can ignite on impact, is made to be used in or with a cartridge, and is not more than 15 mm (⅝ inches) in diameter • Any projectile that can explode on impact, is made to be used in or with a cartridge, and is not more than 15 mm (⅝ inches) in diameter • Any cartridge that can be fired from a shotgun and contains projectiles, known as flechettes, or any similar projectiles

8.2.2 Table 15 - Prohibited Devices

Table 15. Prohibited devices

Prohibited Devices
Individuals cannot acquire prohibited devices. Prohibited devices are regulated under the *Criminal Code*. Depending on the nature of their duties, employees of businesses and carriers, and public officers (police or peace officer, firearms officer, prescribed employee of a federal, provincial or municipal government) may possess prohibited devices. The following are examples of prohibited devices: • Any part of a weapon or accessory of a weapon that is prescribed by regulation to be a prohibited device • A handgun barrel that is equal to or less than 105 mm (4⅛ inches) in length (does not include any handgun barrel that is used in competitions governed by the rules of the *International Shooting Union* and prescribed by regulation) • A device designed to muffle or stop the sound of a firearm (silencers) • A cartridge magazine prescribed by regulation to be a prohibited device • Replica firearms

Refer to the appropriate sections of the *Firearms Act* and *Regulations* for detailed requirements relating to the storage, display, transportation and handling of restricted firearms.

a. **Remember, you are responsible for your firearms 24 hours a day.** Anyone who owns or uses a firearm must meet safe storage, display, transportation and handling requirements. These requirements are set out in the *Storage, Display, Transportation and Handling of Firearms by Individuals Regulations*. All of these are described in this section.

b. Firearms owners and users should always assume that anyone untrained in the safe handling and use of firearms does not know how to handle firearms safely. Fatal incidents or serious accidents could occur from unauthorized access, especially where children are concerned. To prevent this, always store, display, transport and handle firearms and ammunition in accordance with the Regulations.

c. **Remember the law requires that all firearms must be unloaded** except when actually in use.

8.3 Storage

a. A restricted firearm may be stored, only if it meets the following conditions:

   • It is unloaded; and

       • Rendered inoperable by using a secure locking device (see Figure 49) and stored in a securely locked container, receptacle or room that cannot be easily broken open or into, or

       • Stored in a securely locked vault (see Figure 50), safe or room specifically built or adapted for the secure storage of restricted firearms; and

   • Not within easy access to ammunition, unless the ammunition is stored, together with or separately from the firearm, in a securely locked container or receptacle that cannot be easily broken open or into, or a securely locked vault, safe or room specifically built or adapted for the secure storage of restricted firearms.

Figure 49. Cable and trigger locks

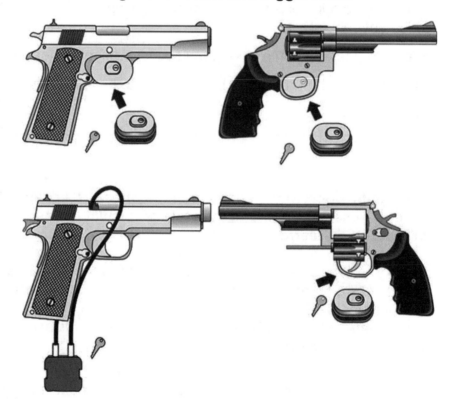

⚠ **Keep in mind that storing ammunition in an unvented container may create an explosive hazard during a fire.**

Figure 50. Storage vault

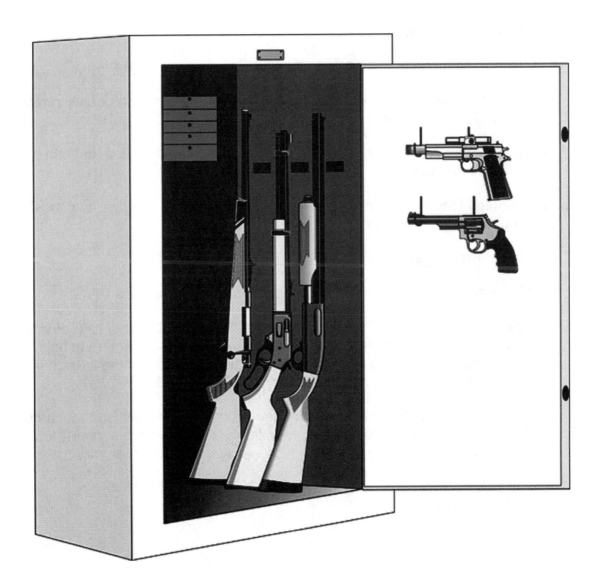

8.4 Display

a. A restricted firearm may be displayed in a dwelling house only under the following conditions:

- It is unloaded; **and**

- Rendered inoperable by using a secure locking device; **and**

- Securely attached to a non-portable structure that cannot be easily removed (see Figure 51); **and**

- Not displayed with and not within easy access to ammunition that can be discharged from it.

b. A restricted firearm may be displayed in a place other than a dwelling house only if it meets the following conditions:

- It is unloaded, **and**

- Rendered inoperable by using a secure locking device; **and**

- Securely attached to a structure by a chain, metal cable or similar device in a manner that the firearm cannot be easily removed; (a firearm may be removed from the display to allow someone to handle it, if the firearm is under the direct supervision of the person displaying it); **and**

- Not displayed with, and not within easy access to, ammunition that can be discharged from it, unless the ammunition is displayed in a securely locked container or receptacle that cannot be easily broken open or into.

Figure 51. Display

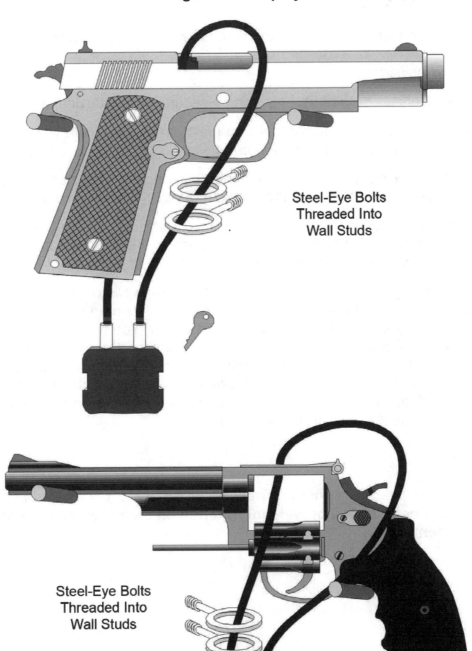

Steel-Eye Bolts
Threaded Into
Wall Studs

Steel-Eye Bolts
Threaded Into
Wall Studs

8.5 Transportation

a. A restricted firearm may be transported only under the following conditions:

- It is unloaded; **and**

  - Rendered inoperable by using a secure locking device; **and**

  - In a locked container that is made of an opaque material and cannot be easily broken open or into or accidentally opened during transportation.

- You may leave the locked container (carrying the restricted firearm) in an unattended vehicle's securely locked trunk or similar compartment.

- If the unattended vehicle does not have a securely locked trunk or similar compartment, lock the vehicle, or the part of the vehicle that contains the container, and leave the locked container out of sight.

b. When transporting your restricted firearm between two or more specific places, you will need an Authorization to Transport. To obtain an Authorization to Transport, you need to contact a firearms officer. You will need to provide the following information: your firearms licence number, the registration certificate number of the firearm to be transported, the frequency, dates and times the firearm will be transported, the place of departure and destination of the transported firearms, and the reason for transporting the firearm. (Please note: provincial/territorial policies may also apply).

If you want to transport firearms on an aircraft, you should first contact the air carrier. They will provide information on their regulations and requirements.

8.6 Handling

a. Before obtaining a restricted firearm, think about how you will transport it home. It is required by regulations that all restricted firearms be transported unloaded and rendered inoperable with a secure locking device. They must also be in a locked opaque case or container (see Figure 52).

b. There are locations where discharging a firearm violates federal or provincial acts and regulations, or municipal bylaws. It may also be an offence to load or handle firearms in these places. You may load a firearm or handle a loaded firearm **only** in a place where it is lawful to discharge it.

Only load a firearm when you intend to use it, and only in an area where it can be safely and legally discharged.

Figure 52. Lockable carrying / storage case

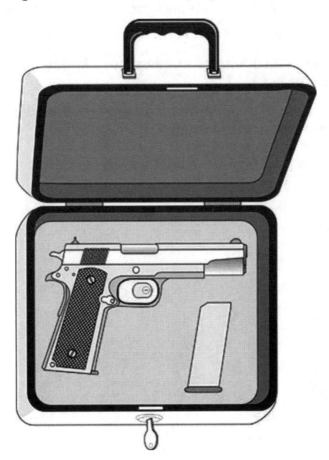

Every person commits an offence who, without lawful excuse, points a firearm at another person, whether the firearm is loaded or unloaded, and is:

1. guilty of an indictable offence and liable to imprisonment for a term not exceeding five years, or

2. guilty of an offence punishable on summary conviction (a fine of $2,000 and/or six months' imprisonment).

Reference: Subsections 87(1) and (2) of Part III of the *Criminal Code*

Every person who stores, displays transports or handles any firearm in a manner contrary to the *Storage, Display, Transportation and Handling of Firearms by Individuals Regulations* is subject to the following:

1. guilty of an indictable offence and liable to imprisonment,

   • in the case of a first offence, for a term not exceeding two years, and

   • in the case of a second or subsequent offence, for a term not exceeding five years; or

2. guilty of an offence punishable on summary conviction (a fine of $2,000 and/or six months' imprisonment).

Reference: Subsections 86(2) and (3) of Part III of the *Criminal Code*

8.7 Table 16 - The Vital Four ACTS of Firearm Safety

Table 16. The vital four ACTS of firearm safety

	The Vital Four ACTS of Firearm Safety
☞	**A**ssume every firearm is loaded. • Regard any firearm as a potential danger.
☞	**C**ontrol the muzzle direction at all times. • Identify the safest available muzzle direction. • Keep the firearm pointed in the safest available direction. • The muzzle of a firearm should not be pointed towards yourself or any other person.
☞	**T**rigger finger must be kept off the trigger and out of the trigger guard. • Resist the temptation to put your finger on the trigger or inside the trigger guard when you pick up a firearm. • Accidental discharge is far more likely to occur if your finger is on the trigger or inside the trigger guard.
☞	**S**ee that the firearm is unloaded - PROVE it safe. • Do not handle the firearm unless you can **PROVE** it safely. • Check to see that both chamber and magazine are empty. Do this every time you handle a firearm, for any reason. • Pass or accept only open and unloaded firearms. This is an important habit to develop.

8.8 PROVE Safe

PROVE it safe:

- **P**oint the firearm in the safest available direction.

- **R**emove all ammunition.

- **O**bserve the chamber.

- **V**erify the feeding path.

- **E**xamine the bore.

The firearm is now unloaded and safe until it leaves the direct control of the person who unloaded and PROVEd it safe.

8.9 Review Questions

1. What are the three common criteria for storing and transporting restricted firearms?

   lock, lock, lock / PAL, ATT, Registration

2. What documents are required to own and transport a restricted firearm to a shooting range?

3. What are the consequences of contravening the *Storage, Display, Transportation and Handling of Firearms by Individuals Regulations*?

   Dual offence

4. Describe the appropriate way to transport a restricted firearm in an unattended vehicle that does not have a trunk?

NOTES:

APPENDIXES

Appendix A: Overview

These Appendixes are provided for general information purposes only. The information contained in this section may be additional to that contained in the course. Information contained in this section will not form part of the written or practical tests.

For legal references, please refer to the actual legislation, namely the *Firearms Act* and its *Regulations*, and Part III of the *Criminal Code*.

Appendix B: Antique Firearms

An antique firearm refers to any firearm manufactured before 1898 that was not designed or redesigned to discharge rim-fire or centre-fire ammunition, plus any other firearm specifically identified as an antique by Regulations. Owners of antique firearms do not need to have a firearms licence or a registration certificate. There are also no restrictions on the transfer of antique firearms. However, antique firearms owners must comply with the requirements found in the *Storage, Display, Transportation and Handling of Firearms by Individuals Regulations*.

Source: Section 84, Part III of the *Criminal Code*, Paragraph 117(h), *Firearms Act*

Appendix C: Buying Ammunition

Any individual wishing to buy ammunition in Canada must have a valid Canadian firearms licence. (Non-residents must have either a confirmed declaration or a temporary borrowing licence to buy ammunition in Canada.)

Appendix D: Legal Definitions

The following definitions are taken from the *Firearms Act* and its *Regulations*, and Part III of the *Criminal Code*.

ammunition: A cartridge containing a projectile designed to be discharged from a firearm and, without restricting the generality of the foregoing, includes a caseless cartridge and a shot shell. *(munitions)*

antique firearm: (1) Any firearm manufactured before 1898 that was not designed to discharge rim-fire or centre-fire ammunition and that has not been redesigned to discharge such ammunition. (2) Any firearm that is prescribed to be an antique firearm. *(arme à feu historique)*

firearm: A barrelled weapon from which any shot, bullet or other projectile can be discharged and that is capable of causing serious bodily injury or death to a person, and includes any frame or receiver of such a barrelled weapon and anything that can be adapted for use as a firearm. *(arme à feu)*

handgun: A firearm that is designed, altered or intended to be aimed and fired by the action of one hand, whether or not it has been redesigned or subsequently altered to be aimed and fired by the action of both hands. *(arme de poing)*

non-restricted firearm: A firearm that is neither a prohibited firearm nor a restricted firearm. *(arme à feu sans restrictions)*

prohibited ammunition: Ammunition, or a projectile of any kind, that is prescribed to be prohibited ammunition. *(munitions prohibées)*

prohibited device: (1) Any component or part of a weapon, or any accessory for use with a weapon, that is prescribed to be a prohibited device. (2) A handgun barrel that is equal to or less than 105 mm in length, but does not include any such handgun barrel that is prescribed, where the handgun barrel is for use in international sporting competitions governed by the rules of the International Shooting Union (3) A device or contrivance designed or intended to muffle or stop the sound or report of a firearm (4) A cartridge magazine that is prescribed to be a prohibited device. (5) A replica firearm. *(dispositif prohibé)*

prohibited firearm: (1) A handgun that has a barrel equal to or less than 105 mm in length, or is designed or adapted to discharge a 25- or 32-calibre cartridge, but does not include any such handgun that is prescribed, where the handgun is for use in international sporting competitions governed by the rules of the International Shooting Union. (2) A firearm that is adapted from a rifle or shotgun, whether by sawing, cutting or any other alteration, and that, as so adapted, is less than 660 mm in length, or is 660 mm or greater in length and has a barrel less than 457 mm in length. (3) An automatic firearm, whether or not it has been altered to discharge only one projectile with one pressure of the trigger. (5) Any firearm that is prescribed to be a prohibited firearm. *(arme à feu prohibée)*

replica firearm: Any device that is designed or intended to exactly resemble, or to resemble with near precision, a firearm, and that itself is not a firearm, but does not include any such device that is designed or intended to exactly resemble, or to resemble with near precision, an antique firearm. *(réplique)*

restricted firearm: (1) A handgun that is not a prohibited firearm. (2) A firearm that is not a prohibited firearm, has a barrel less than 470 mm in length, and is capable of discharging centre-fire ammunition in a semi-automatic manner. (3) A firearm that is designed or adapted to be fired when reduced to a length of less than 660 mm by folding, telescoping or otherwise. (4) A firearm of any other kind that is prescribed to be a restricted firearm. *(arme à feu à autorisation restreinte)*

secure locking device: A device that can only be opened or released by the use of an electronic, magnetic or mechanical key or by setting the device in accordance with an alphabetical or numerical combination; and that, when applied to a firearm, prevents the firearm from being discharged. *(dispositif de verrouillage sécuritaire)*

unattended: In respect of a vehicle, means that the vehicle is not under the direct and immediate supervision of a person who is 18 years of age or older or to whom a licence has been issued under the Act. *(non surveillé)*

unloaded: In respect of a firearm, means that any propellant, projectile or cartridge that can be discharged from the firearm is not contained in the breech or firing chamber of the firearm nor in the cartridge magazine attached to or inserted into the firearm. *(non chargée)*

vehicle: Any conveyance that is used for transportation by water, land or air. *(véhicule)*

Appendix E: Personal Firearms Inventory (example)

MAKE:

MODEL:

SERIAL NO:

FIREARM IDENTIFICATION NUMBER:

MANUFACTURER:

BARREL LENGTH:

CALIBRE / GAUGE:

REGISTRATION CERTIFICATE NUMBER:

PURCHASED FROM:

DATE OF PURCHASE:

VALUE:

DISTINGUISHING MARKS:

ACCESSORIES (case, grips, etc.):

Appendix F: Replica Firearms

A replica firearm is designed or intended to exactly, or almost exactly, resemble a firearm, but itself is not a firearm. Under Part III of the *Criminal Code*, a replica firearm is a prohibited device. Owners of replica firearms do not need to have a firearms licence or a registration certificate. However, replica firearms owners must comply with the transportation requirements found in the *Storage, Display, Transportation and Handling of Firearms by Individuals Regulations.*

Source: Section 84, Part III of the *Criminal Code*, Paragraph 117(i), *Firearms Act*

Appendix G: Reporting Lost or Stolen Firearms, Licences, etc.

Where a firearm or other weapon is lost or stolen, or a licence, registration certificate or authorization is lost or stolen—it must be reported.

A person commits an offence if after having lost a firearm, a prohibited weapon, a restricted weapon, a prohibited device, any prohibited ammunition, an authorization, a licence or a registration certificate, or having had it stolen, does not report the loss or theft with reasonable dispatch to a peace officer, firearms officer, or Chief Firearms Officer.

Similarly, a person commits an offence, if on finding a firearm, a prohibited weapon, a restricted weapon, a prohibited device, or any prohibited ammunition, does not report the find, or deliver the item, with reasonable dispatch to a peace officer, firearms officer, or Chief Firearms Officer. This offence does not extend to documents, specifically an authorization, a licence or a registration certificate.

Commission of either offence is punishable on summary conviction or by indictment.

Source: Section 105, Part III of the *Criminal Code*

Appendix H: Visual Range Signals & Devices

Flags or Signs: Typically a red flag flown at or near the entrance to the property. It serves to warn people that live fire may occur at any time and that shooters are actively using one or more ranges. Some clubs have individual "in use" flags for each range.

Down Range Activity Signals: Typically a red light, rope, or red flag at the entrance to the down range area. Red means stop! Do not go down range. A few clubs use a green flag or light to indicate it is safe to go down range. This display should NOT be visible from the shooting positions! Some ranges fly "down range" red flags to show it is NOT safe to discharge firearms; this is potentially confusing unless the flag cannot be seen by people in the down range area.

Shooting Line Activity Signals: Typically a red light, a red flashing light, a red flag, or a baffle clearly visible to the shooter when in the shooting position. Red means stop shooting! On some indoor ranges, the white lights that illuminate the firing line are dimmed and red illumination supplied. This display should NOT be positioned or used in a manner to be confused with the red signal at the entry to the down range area. Some ranges fly "down range" green flags to show that the range is safe for live fire; this is potentially confusing unless the flag cannot be seen by people in the down range area.

Appendix I: Gun Collector

The *Firearms Act* recognizes that collecting firearms is a legitimate reason for owning firearms. The rules on gun collecting apply to restricted firearms and to "grandfathered" prohibited handguns with barrel lengths of 105 mm or less, or 25 and 32 calibre. In order to collect grandfathered handguns, an individual must have registered one such handgun as of December 1, 1998 and then continuously thereafter maintained a registration for one such handgun. In order to qualify as a gun collector, a person must,

- have knowledge of the historical, technical or scientific characteristics of the firearms that are part of a collection;

- give signed consent to periodic inspections of the area where the collection is stored; and

- comply with safe storage, display, handling and transportation standards.

When a person acquires a restricted firearm or prohibited handgun, or when he or she renews their firearms licence, the Chief Firearms Officer must determine whether the firearm is being acquired, or firearms already in possession are for the purpose of gun collection.

Source: Sections 67, 28 and 30, *Firearms Act*

Appendix J: Firearms Licences

Under the *Firearms Act* anyone wishing to possess, borrow, buy, inherit or otherwise acquire firearms must have a valid Firearms Licence.

The *Firearms Act* and *Firearms Licences Regulations* set out the following types of individual firearms licences:

- Possession Only Licence
- Possession and Acquisition Licence
- Minors Possession Licence
- Non-resident Sixty-day Possession Licence (Borrowed Firearms)
- Non-resident Firearm Declaration (Confirmation of Importation of a Firearm by a Non-resident)

Requirements for obtaining firearms licences are the same across Canada. Most, if not all of these licences are available on-line on the CAFC Internet website at: www.cfc-cafc.gc.ca.

Possession Only Licence (POL)
This type of licence authorizes the continued possession of firearms already owned, but does not permit the acquiring of additional firearms. This licence is no longer available to new licence applicants. Existing POL holders may renew their licence as long as they continue to lawfully and continuously possess at least one firearm in the particular class.

Possession and Acquisition Licence (PAL)
This type of licence is required for anyone wishing to acquire firearms, whether for the first time or in addition to the firearms already owned. An individual must successfully complete the Canadian Firearms Safety Course and/or tests to obtain this licence for non-restricted firearms. To obtain this licence for restricted firearms and/or prohibited firearms an individual must also successfully complete the Canadian Restricted Firearms Safety Course and/or tests. There is a minimum 28-day waiting period for this licence, unless the applicant already holds a valid POL, PAL or Minors Possession Licence.

Appendix K: Transferring Firearms

Sections 22 and 23 of the *Firearms Act* set out a number of conditions that must be satisfied by both parties involved in the transfer of a firearm before the transfer is authorized. In addition, there are a number of conditions that apply in the *Conditions of Transferring Firearms and Other Weapons Regulations*. These obligations apply to each and every transfer of firearms, regardless of the class of firearm.

The following outlines the information that must be provided when individuals transfer (sell, barter, or give away) firearms.

Transferor's Obligations
An individual who wants to transfer a firearm must:

1. be reasonably sure that the transferee does not have a mental illness which would give rise to public safety concerns;

2. be reasonably sure that the transferee is not impaired by alcohol or drugs;

3. require the transferee to show a licence which authorizes the transferee to acquire and possess the particular class of firearm;

4. be satisfied that the licence shown authorizes the transferee to acquire and possess the particular class of firearm;

5. inform a Chief of Firearms Officer of the transfer and obtain his or her authorization;

6. ensure that the following conditions (subsection 2(1) of the *Conditions of Transferring Firearms and Other Weapons Regulations*) are complied with;

   • provide the Chief Firearms Officer with the transferor's and transferee's name and address;

   • provide the Chief Firearms Officer with the transferor's and transferee's licence numbers; and

   • inform the Chief Firearms Officer of the class of firearm being transferred.

Transferee's Obligations

In order for a transfer to be authorized, the individual to whom the firearms will be transferred must:

1. hold a possession and acquisition licence for the particular class of firearm;

2. ensure that a new registration certificate is issued by the Registrar;

3. for the transfer of restricted firearms and prohibited handguns (pre-December 1, 1998) only,

   - inform the Chief Firearms Officer why he or she needs to acquire the firearms (the protection of life, lawful profession or occupation, target practice or competition, or part of a gun collection);

   - if the transferee is acquiring the firearm to form part of a gun collection, he or she will have to provide the Chief Firearms Officer with:

     - information regarding his or her knowledge of characteristics which relate or distinguish the restricted firearms or handguns that he or she possesses;

     - signed consent to reasonably conducted periodic inspections of the area where the collection is kept; and

     - details of his or her knowledge of safe storage requirements for restricted firearms or prohibited handguns.

4. for the transfer of prohibited firearms only, provide the Chief Firearms Officer with the number of the registration certificate issued to him or her.

Before authorizing a transfer, the Chief Firearms Officer must determine whether or not the transfer will affect the safety of others. If the transfer is authorized, the Chief Firearms Officer will issue a unique transfer authorization number to both parties. Where transfers are completed by telephone, the transfer number provided to both parties will serve as a confirmation of the transfer and as a temporary registration certificate until a new registration certificate is sent in the mail.

Effective January 1, 2003, registration information will have to be verified by an authorized verifier. The transferor will be asked to provide evidence that the information concerning the firearm has been verified by an authorized verifier. Verification has to be done only once and the registration certificate will indicate whether or not the firearm data has been verified.

GLOSSARY

A

action: The moving parts of a firearm that load, fire, extract and eject ammunition.

action release: The part of a firearm that unlatches or opens the action to give access to the chamber.

airgun: A firearm that uses compressed air or carbon dioxide to propel a projectile.

ammunition: See under **Appendix D: Legal Definitions**.

antique firearm: See under **Appendix D: Legal Definitions**.

aperture sight: A rear sight with a hole for viewing the target. Also known as a peep sight.

automatic: An action that fires cartridges in rapid succession during one sustained pressure of the trigger.

B

ball:
a). A lead projectile fired by black powder firearms.
b). Full metal jacket ammunition.

ballistics: The study of projectiles in flight and what affects them. This means the barrel, in flight and within the target, including trajectory, force, impact and penetration.

barrel: The metal tube of a firearm. The bullet, shot or projectile accelerates down it when the firearm is fired.

barrel length: The distance from the muzzle to the chamber, including the chamber itself. This measurement does not include accessories or barrel extensions like flash suppressors or muzzle brakes. The barrel length of a revolver is the distance from the muzzle to the breech end immediately in front of the cylinder.

BB gun: A type of air gun designed to use spherical steel BB pellets.

big bore: A rifle shooting term that refers to centre-fire firearms or ammunition.

black powder: A finely ground powder, mainly used in muzzleloaders and antique cartridge firearms. The basic ingredients are salt-petre (potassium nitrate), charcoal (carbon) and sulphur.

blueing or bluing: An oxidation (rust) process applied to firearm metal parts. Controlled by applying oil that mixes with the nitrates used in the process. The oil prevents further rusting by sealing the metal. This gives the metal a blue/black colour that resulted in the name "bluing".

boat tail: The tapered rear end of some bullets, used to increase ballistic efficiency at long range.

bolt: A steel rod-like assembly that moves back and forth in an action, sealing the cartridge in the chamber during firing.

bolt action: For registration purposes, a repeating firearm that has a magazine and in which the breech bolt or closure device operates in line with the bore; manually operated by a permanent projection or handle attached to the bolt or closure device.

bolt face: The forward end of the bolt that supports the base of the cartridge.

bore: The inside of the barrel of a firearm excluding the chamber. The channel through which the bullet or other projectile is fired from the gun.

bore diameter: The measurement from one side of the bore to the other. See also **rifling; calibre.**

breech: The rear end of the barrel into which the ammunition is loaded. See also **chamber.**

breechblock: The part in the breech mechanism that locks the action against the firing of the cartridge.

breechloader: A firearm loaded through the breech.

buckshot: Large lead pellets used in shotgun shells.

bullet: A projectile designed to be fired from a rifled barrel.

butt: The rear end of a rifle or shotgun (the portion that rests against the shoulder.) In a handgun, the bottom part of the grip.

butt stock: In long guns, the part of the stock which extends from the receiver to the butt.

C

calibre: A measurement in metric or imperial units to describe the inside diameter of the barrel of a rifled firearm. Calibre is also used to describe the diameter of a projectile in a cartridge.

cap: See **percussion cap.**

carbine: A light short-barrelled rifle.

cartridge: A complete unit of ammunition consisting of a case, primer, powder and a projectile. Modern cartridges are generally classified into two categories: centre-fire and rim-fire. See also **shell.**

cartridge magazine: A device or container from which ammunition may be fed into the firing chamber of
a firearm. Part 4 of the *Regulations Prescribing Certain Firearms and other Weapons, Components, and Parts of Weapons, Accessories, Cartridge Magazines, Ammunition and Projectiles as Prohibited or Restricted* sets out the limit for the number of cartridges permitted for different types of magazines. The two common types are box-type magazine and tubular magazine.

case: Also called casing. The container of a cartridge. It is usually of brass or other metal when used for rifles and handguns. When used for shotguns, it is usually of paper or plastic with a metal head, and is more often called a hull.

cease-fire:
a). As a verb - The command to stop shooting, unload firearms and step behind the cease-fire line.
b). As a noun - Time or period of range inactivity while targets are changed or other activities are conducted.

centre-fire: A cartridge with its primer located in the centre of the base of the case.

chainfiring: The term used to describe the dangerous result of not using grease over the balls used in a black powder revolver. When the primary cylinder is fired, lack of grease on the other cylinders may cause them to discharge before they are lined up with the barrel.

chamber:
a). The portion at the breech end of the barrel. The cartridge is placed in the chamber ready for firing. A revolver is multi-chambered.
b). To place a cartridge in the barrel.

charge:
a). The amount, by weight, of the powder in a cartridge.
b). In the case of black powder, the amount, by volume, of the powder used.
c). To fill a magazine with cartridges.

Chief Firearms Officer: The person in authority in a province or territory responsible for licences, authorizations to transport, authorizations to carry and other functions related to the administration of the *Firearms Act* and its *Regulations.*

choke: Narrowing at the muzzle end of a shotgun barrel that determines the shot pattern.

cleaning kit: A set of specialized accessories used to clean and maintain a firearm.

clip: An incorrect term used to describe a magazine.

cock: To set the action into position for firing. On some firearms, the action has an intermediate position called half cock. On muzzleloading firearms, the cock holds the flint or match.

coking: The burning of black powder residue with much heat and little smoke.

comb: The upper edge of a rifle or shotgun stock where the holder's cheek rests.

conical bullet: A cylindrical shaped bullet with a cone shaped tip.

core: The part of a bullet that is covered by a jacket, i.e. the centre of a bullet.

corrosion: The gradual eating away of the metal parts of a firearm caused by rust or other chemical reactions.

crimp: The portion of a cartridge or shell case that is bent inward to hold the bullet or shot in place.

cross-bolt safety: A device that blocks the firing mechanism of a firearm.

cross-hairs: The sighting lines in a telescopic sight.

cylinder: The part of a revolver that rotates and in which chambers are bored to hold cartridges. It combines the functions of magazine, feed system and firing chamber.

cylinder bore: A shotgun barrel having the same diameter throughout, i.e. without choke. It is used to fire solid slugs.

D

dangerous range: The maximum distance at which a projectile will travel. See also **range.**

deactivated firearm: A deactivated firearm is one that has been rendered permanently inoperable. The standards for deactivated firearms are determined by the RCMP/CAFC.

dominant eye: See **master eye**.

double action: An action that cocks and fires with a complete pull of the trigger.

double action only: An action that cannot fire in a single action mode.

double-action revolver: A revolver that both cocks and fires with a complete pull of the trigger.

double-barrel: A firearm with two barrels, either side-by-side or one over the other.

down range: The direction from the shooting position towards the target on a range. See also **range**.

dry firing: Firing of an unloaded firearm to practice handling and shooting techniques. This can damage some types of actions, particularly rim-fire.

dummy ammunition: Inactive ammunition used for practising handling of firearms. It has no primers or propellants. See also **live ammunition**.

E

effective range: The maximum distance for a shooter at which he or she can confidently hit the target. Also refers to the useful range of the projectile(s). See also **range.**

ejector: The mechanism that expels the cartridge or case from the firearm.

extraction: The removal of a cartridge or case from the chamber of a firearm.

F

feed: The action of moving a fresh cartridge into the chamber.

feeding path: The path a cartridge follows within an action.

field stripping: Taking apart a firearm for regular maintenance and cleaning.

firearm: See under **Appendix D: Legal Definitions.**

firing pin: The part of the breech mechanism that strikes the primer of the cartridge.

flash suppressor: Muzzle attachment designed to cool emergent gases and prevent or reduce muzzle flash.

flat-nosed bullet: A bullet with a flattened front end. It is used mainly in cartridges designed for rifles with tubular magazines.

flechette: A small dart stabilized by fins. It is encased in a discarding sabot (case) and loaded into a shotgun shell. Usually, one shell will contain a number of flechettes. This type of ammunition is prohibited.

flintlock: The gunlock of early firearms in which flint is struck against steel. This causes sparks to ignite the powder charge.

floor plate: The metal plate at the bottom of some cartridge magazines. (The floor plate is usually hinged at the front and held by a release spring located just ahead of the trigger guard.)

follow-through: Staying in the same position after squeezing the trigger or continuing the swing in firing at a moving target. This helps to shoot accurately.

follower: The part of a magazine between the spring and the ammunition. You must be able to see or feel the follower to know the magazine is empty. See also **magazine follower.**

forcing cone: In smooth bore and revolver barrels, a cone that joins the chamber to the bore. It assists the passage of the projectile(s) into the bore. Also called a throat.

forearm/fore-stock: The forward part of a one or two piece stock. It is sometimes called a slide on pump action firearms.

frizzen: The metal arm of a flintlock mechanism. The flint strikes the frizzen to create sparks in the flash pan. It is also called a battery.

full cock: The position of the hammer or striker when the firearm is ready to fire.

full metal jacket: A bullet with a jacket, usually of harder metal, encasing the core. It is also called a hard-point bullet. Used in ball ammunition.

G

gauge: The measurement of the diameter of a shotgun bore.

grain: A unit of weight (7,000 grains equal one pound) commonly used to measure the weight of ammunition components. Black powder and its substitutes are measured in grains by volume. Modern powders are measured by weight.

grip: The small portion of the stock gripped by the trigger hand.

grooves: See **rifling.**

H

half cock: A safety feature on some firearms. When the hammer is pulled back half-way, it cannot be fired by squeezing the trigger.

hammer: The part of the action that drives the firing pin forward.

handgun: See under **Appendix D: Legal Definitions.**

hangfire: A malfunction causing a delay in firing a cartridge after the firing pin has struck the primer.

high power: A term applied to the first smokeless powder cartridges with velocities of approximately 609.6 m/s (2,000 ft./s).

high power rifle: Generally, a firearm that uses centre-fire ammunition.

holding: The action of keeping the sights on the target while squeezing the trigger.

hollow point: A bullet with a hollow at the tip (nose) that makes it expand more on impact.

hull: The outer covering or casing of a shotgun shell.

I

No applicable entry.

J

jacket: The outer covering over the inner metal core of a bullet.

K

kick: See **recoil**.

L

lands: See **rifling**.

leading: Particles from shot or bullets that stick to the metal surface of the bore. This is due to heat or friction.

lever action:
a). An action operated by a lever located underneath it. (A secondary purpose of the lever is to serve as a trigger guard).
b). For registration purposes, a repeating firearm that has a magazine and a breech mechanism cycled by an external lever, usually below the receiver or frame.

line of sight: An imaginary straight line from the shooter's eye to the target; usually through the sights.

live ammunition: Ammunition containing primers and propellants capable of firing bullets or other projectiles.

load: To prepare a firearm for firing by inserting ammunition into it.

loading gate: The hinged cover over the opening through which cartridges are inserted into the magazine or chamber.

loading port: The opening through which cartridges are inserted into the magazine or chamber.

lock: The firing mechanism of a muzzleloader. In firearms that are loaded through the breech, the lock is both the firing mechanism and breech-sealing assembly.

long gun: Generic term used to describe rifles and shotguns.

M

magazine: See **cartridge magazine.**

magazine cut off: Disengages magazine feed from firearm.

magazine follower: Spring-loaded platform in a magazine. It pushes cartridges or shells to the feeding position. When checking that a firearm is completely unloaded, the magazine follower should be clearly in view. This is especially important with tubular magazines.

magazine release: A button or switch that allows for the removal of a magazine from the firearm.

magnum:
a). A cartridge or shell with a larger capacity or with a higher velocity than average (e.g. 3.5-inch Magnum shot shell, .300 Winchester Magnum rifle, .44 Remington Magnum handgun). Firearms that use magnum ammunition may also be called magnum.
b). A marketing term used by manufacturers which may or may not indicate greater power or range.

mainspring: A strong spring which activates the striker or hammer of a firearm.

malfunction: The failure of a firearm to work properly. This can be caused by a jam or stoppage, or a mechanical or structural failure.

master eye: The stronger eye; the eye through which a person usually views an object as when sighting a firearm.

match/wick: A long cord soaked in saltpetre, which burns slowly. Used to ignite powder in early firearms.

matchlock: A firearm action that uses a serpentine or S-shaped piece of metal to hold a smouldering match. The burning match contacts the priming powder in the pan to ignite the charge.

metallic cartridge: A cartridge with a metallic case. In contrast, early cartridge cases were made of linen, paper, etc.

mid-range: The point in the trajectory halfway between the muzzle and the target.

Mini-ball or Minie ball: A cylindrical shaped bullet used in muzzleloaders. It has a pointed tip and a hollow base that spreads as it is fired.

misfire: The failure of a cartridge to fire after the firing pin has struck the primer. Do not confuse with hangfire, which is a delay in firing.

mushroom: The shape many soft-point bullets become when they expand upon impact.

musket: An early smoothbore shoulder firearm.

muzzle: The opening at the end of the barrel from which the bullet or shot emerges.

muzzle brake: A device attached to the muzzle that softens the recoil of the firearm. Also known as a compensator.

muzzleloader: A firearm that is loaded through the muzzle.

N

non-restricted firearm: See under **Appendix D: Legal Definitions.**

O

open sight: A type of firearm sight, usually with a "V" or "U" notch in the rear sight. See also **sight.**

over-and-under: A firearm, usually a shotgun, with two barrels placed one over the other.

P

pan: The small container located on the side or top of a matchlock, wheel lock or flintlock firearm used to hold the priming powder.

patch:
a). A small piece of leather or cloth that is greased and placed around a bullet before ramming it down the barrel of a muzzleloader.
b). A piece of cloth drawn through the bore of a firearm to clean it.

patch box: A small compartment in the butt of a muzzleloader used to store patches or other small items.

pattern: Distribution of the shot in a shotgun charge. This is measured at a standard distance of 40 yards and in a 30-inch circle.

peep sight: A rear sight with a hole through which the target is viewed. Also known as an aperture sight.

pellet: Small round projectiles loaded into shotgun shells. Usually referred to as shot. Also a lead projectile used in some air guns.

penetration: The depth that a projectile travels into a target before it stops.

percussion cap: A small metal explosive filled cup that is placed over the nipple of a percussion firearm.

pistol: A small hand-held firearm.

powder: The general term for any propellant used in firearms which burns upon ignition. The two major types are black powder (an explosive) and smokeless powder (a propellant).

powder burn: Charring caused by gunshot residue.

powder charge: The amount of powder by weight in the case of smokeless powder, and by volume, in the case of black powder.

prime: In the case of a black powder firearm, to place powder on the pan or percussion cap on the nipple. Also, to place a primer in a cartridge case.

primer: The overall term for the priming compound, cup and anvil which, when struck, ignites the powder charge.

primer pop: The sound of only the primer discharging due to no or grossly inadequate charge of powder in the cartridge.

prohibited ammunition: See under **Appendix D: Legal Definitions.**

prohibited device: See under **Appendix D: Legal Definitions.**

prohibited firearm: See under **Appendix D: Legal Definitions.**

projectile: A bullet or shot in flight after firing from a firearm.

propellant: The chemical substance which, when ignited, propels the projectile. Also called powder.

pull-through: The cord used to pull a bore brush or cleaning patch through the bore of a firearm.

pump action:
a). An action that is operated by moving the fore-end in a motion parallel to the bore.
b). For registration purposes, a repeating firearm that has a magazine and is manually set in motion usually parallel to the barrel; also called slide action or trombone action.

Q

No applicable entry.

R

ramrod: A wood or metal rod used to push the patch and bullet down the barrel of a muzzleloader.

range:
a). The distance travelled by a projectile from firearm to target.
b). A projectile's maximum travelling distance.
c). An area or facility designed for the safe shooting of firearms.
d). Dangerous range: the maximum distance at which a projectile will travel.
e). Effective range: the greatest distance a projectile will travel with accuracy.

receiver: A firearm's metal frame that generally contains the breech, locking and loading mechanisms. Normally the serial number is on the receiver. Also called the frame.

recoil: The backward movement of a firearm when it is fired. Also called kick.

replica firearm: See under **Appendix D: Legal Definitions.**

restricted firearm: See under **Appendix D: Legal Definitions.**

revolver:

a). A repeating handgun that has a revolving cylinder with a series of chambers. The cylinder may revolve in either direction, depending on the manufacturer.

b). For registration purposes, a firearm, usually a handgun, that has a revolving cylinder with a series of chambers, and is discharged successively by the same firing mechanism. The chamber may revolve in either direction depending on the manufacturer.

revolving action: An action with a revolving cylinder containing a number of cartridge chambers. One chamber at a time lines up with the barrel.

ricochet: The redirection of a projectile after impact, usually with a hard surface. For example, a bullet bouncing off a rock.

rifle: A shoulder firearm with a rifled bore. Designed to fire one projectile at a time. See also **rifling.**

rifled slug: A large, single projectile with spiral grooves used in shotguns.

rifling: Spiral grooves inside the barrel. Rifling causes the bullet to spin, increasing its accuracy and range. The depressed portions of the rifling are called grooves and the raised portions are called lands.

rim: The edge on the base of a cartridge case. The rim is the part of the case that the extractor grips to remove the cartridge from the chamber.

rim-fire: A cartridge that has its primer located inside the rim of the case. See also **cartridge.**

rod: A rod used for cleaning a firearm. It is used to check for obstructions prior to loading the firearm. It may also be referred to as a ramrod, proving stick or dummy rod.

round: One shot fired by a firearm. It is also a complete item of ammunition or a cartridge that has all the components needed to fire one shot.

round-nose bullet: A bullet with a rounded nose.

S

sabot: A plastic sleeve that holds a slug that is smaller than the bore diameter of a firearm. It is used mainly in shotguns and muzzleloading firearms.

safety: A device that blocks the firing mechanism of a firearm.

scope: See **sight.**

sear: Part of the firing mechanism linked to the trigger. The sear holds the hammer, firing pin or striker in the cocked position until the trigger is squeezed.

secure locking device: See under **Appendix D: Legal Definitions**.

semi-automatic:
a). An action which fires, extracts, ejects, chambers and cocks with each separate pull of the trigger.
b). For registration purposes, a repeating firearm requiring that the trigger be pulled for each shot fired and which uses the energy of the discharge to perform part of the operating cycle; sometimes called auto-loading or self-loading actions.

semi-wad cutter: A cylindrical bullet with a short truncated cone at the nose. Often used for paper target shooting.

shell: A complete unit of ammunition consisting of a hull, primer, powder, wad and projectile(s) for use in shotguns.

shotgun: A shoulder firearm with a smooth bore designed to fire multiple pellets called shot, or a single projectile called a slug.

shotgun shell: A cartridge used in a shotgun. It contains multiple shot pellets or a single projectile called a slug.

side by side: A firearm, usually a shotgun, with two barrels placed side by side.

sight: A firearm device, either mechanical or optical, that helps the shooter aim accurately.

single action: An action that releases the hammer from a cocked position when the trigger is pulled. Usually found on handguns.

single action revolver: A revolver that requires the hammer to be cocked manually. Pressing the trigger will not cause it to fire until this is done.

single shot: For registration purposes, a single-barrel firearm that is manually loaded and has no magazine-feed device.

slide safety: A device that blocks the firing mechanism of a firearm.

sling: A strap used to carry and aid in aiming a rifle.

slug: A large single projectile used in shotguns. See also **rifled slug.**

small bore: Generally refers to a .22-calibre firearm or rim-fire ammunition.

smokeless powder: Propellant powder used in modern firearms.

smooth bore: A firearm with a bore that is not rifled, such as a shotgun.

soft-point bullet: A bullet with a partial jacket exposing a portion of the lead core at the nose.

spent bullet: A bullet near the end of its flight that has lost nearly all its energy. Despite a loss in energy, spent bullets can still penetrate targets.

spire-point bullet: A bullet with a cone-shaped nose.

stock: The part of a rifle or shotgun used in holding the firearm against the shoulder when firing.

T

tang safety: A device that blocks the firing mechanism of a firearm.

telescopic sight: See **sight.**

trajectory: The path a projectile takes during flight.

trigger: The part of the firearm mechanism that releases the part of the action that fires the cartridge.

trigger guard: The metal loop around the trigger made to protect it and prevent accidentally touching the trigger.

U

unattended: See under **Appendix D: Legal Definitions**

unloaded: See under **Appendix D: Legal Definitions.**

V

vehicle: See under **Appendix D: Legal Definitions**

velocity: The speed at which a projectile travels in a given direction.

W

wad: A paper fibre or plastic disc used to separate the powder charge from the shot or slug, to seal propellant gases behind the charge, and to hold the shot together in the barrel.

wad-cutter: A cylindrical bullet with a sharp, shouldered, nearly flat nose. It is designed to cut paper targets cleanly so they can be scored accurately.

wheel lock: An early firearm mechanism. A wheel with serrated edges is spun against a piece of iron pyrite. This sends sparks into the pan to ignite the charge.

wing safety: A device that blocks the firing mechanism of a firearm.

X

No applicable entry.

Y

No applicable entry.

Z

No applicable entry.